What If...

We Are Not All HERE,

'Cause We Are Not All THERE?

My Spiritual name is:

Joy Child of the Universe

Copyright © 2023 Joy Child of the Universe

Published and distributed in the United States by: Amazon, www.amazon.com

Distributed in the Canada by: Amazon, www.amazon.ca

Distributed in the Europe by: Amazon, www.amazon.co.uk

All rights reserved. No part of this book may be reproduced by any mechanical, photographic, or electronic process, or in the form of a phonographic recording; nor may it be stored in a retrieval system, transmitted, or otherwise be copied for public or private use – other than for "fair use" as brief quotations embodied in articles and reviews without prior written permission of the Author.

The Author of this book does not dispense medical advice or prescribe the use of any technique as a form of treatment for physical or medical problems without the advice of a physician, either directly or indirectly. The intent of the Author is only to offer information of a general nature to help you in your quest for emotional, mental, physical, and spiritual well-being. In the even you use any of the information in this book for yourself, which is your constitutional right; the author assumes no responsibility for your actions.

Copyright © 2023 Joy Child of the Universe

All rights reserved.

ISBN: 13-979-8-3001-6649-6

What If...We Are Not All HERE,

DEDICATION

We dedicate this book to every being who has questions about the meaning of life. There may be some questions that you have wondered about, or maybe a new point of view.

I say "WE" because, as the collective that we all truly are, we all come from one Source, and we will all return to one Source. Therefore, we are all one in the same, just different aspects of the one Source.

This book is lovingly dedicated to the memory of my closest and greatest teachers in this time, my great-grand parents Marie and Fritzy (Fred), grand parents Gloria and Teunis, Hazel and Lorne, and my dad Brian.

I would also like to thank my close family members, especially my mom Verna: you have always been my rock; my partner Ben who has always been by my side for the past 25+ years, my former boss and Publisher Carol Uchytil (with Heart Lines Media) for all your Spiritual guidance and friendship, Patty LaPointe for all her help with the cover; Jo Turley for all your help with making this book possible; to all the mentors that have been walking in and out of my life; my many friends, and even more acquaintances who have popped into and out of my life. You have provided me with a plethora of experiences, understandings, and some very questionable ethical situations, all for my growth and spiritual advancement. I am very grateful to be blessed throughout this lifetime, by others who have helped me along the way.

'Cause We Are Not All THERE.

CONTENTS

	Introduction	i
1	History	1
2	Spirituality	Pg 33
3	The Ego	Pg 91
4	Religion	Pg 99
5	Government & Politics	Pg 113

Dearest Gloria

Thank-you for your Support.

Love & Light
Joy Child
of the Universe

Cell # 403-848-3549.

Introduction

When I started writing this book, I was focused on writing about my life, my experiences, and my perceptions, all the moments that have made some profound memories, and some not so wonderful memories. The entire process of this book has taken many years to formulate and put together, along with some updated information that has been recently documented and published.

The title of this book was supposed to be "I Am Not All Here, 'Cause I Am Not All There," I have been saying these words for as long as I can recall. Then one morning, as I was waking up, a little voice in my head said, "There are millions of possibilities and millions of probabilities, so why don't you write about all the "What If" that you can come up with." Now, the reason for my statement is: since I was in my early years, I have felt like I have one foot grounded to our Mother Earth, while at the same time, my other foot is in the air, or as some would put it, in the Heavens.

I thought that this was a great idea, and this is how the book started. I have written my questions regarding History, Spirituality, Ego, Religion, Governments and Politics from my perspective and research and the information that I have understood since childhood. Well, here they are in black and white.

This book has been created as an interactive book that helps with understanding your truths. We have left some room on the pages for you to put down your own perspectives and thoughts. Maybe some will hit home for you, some you might put aside for later. Either way, our intention is to get everyone to start thinking, wondering, recalling, and pondering all the possibilities and probabilities in your life circumstances. What is the story of your life? Why are you here? What makes you be who you are?

What If...We Are Not All HERE,

I have noticed more and more that as we become more involved in the computer age, there are fewer people, especially our young ones who really don't have to think or ask questions about life anymore. Everything can be downloaded as information off the web.

I have always asked questions throughout this lifetime. I was informed by my family in my youth that I was asking too many questions and disrupting our class at Sunday school, so they asked my grandfather to leave me at home. So, this makes me wonder, why have we all been programmed to stifle our questioning?

With this book, I have added some of my perspectives according to my experiences and thoughts, information that flows through me; these are my understandings and my perspectives only. You may or may not agree and I am okay with that. I understand that each and every being deserves to understand what their deepest feelings and truths are.

If for some reason, some of my questions or answers offend you, I would suggest you take a deeper look within yourself for your own answers. Our intention is to open your heart and mind to connect with your higher-self, your life-force, or whatever you want to call it.

We all use our 5 senses differently. That is partly why we are Individuals and Unique. There may be many moments when there is a group of people who respond in very similar ways, but at the same time, still differently.

'Cause We Are Not All THERE.

If the answers are coming to you or through you, please write them down in a journal. As you start asking question, more and more questions seem to rise up from the depths of your being. I love it. Things to ponder: are you right, are you wrong? This really doesn't matter, from what I understanding, there really isn't any right or wrong, there just is. Whatever may be right for you may not be for another. We are here to be okay with that, and it is just a part of our language so that we may learn and grow. Reach for the stars, muscle test, research, find your perspective or point of view.

Over years of studying and practicing Metaphysics I have read many books regarding past-lives, channeling, various hands-on healing modalities, ancient philosophy, shamanism and some Native history, Buddhism, Theta Healing, Light and Color Therapy, Tarot Cards, Remote Viewing, Mythology, Astral Travel, Crystal Therapy and more. The list can go on and on. I have studied everything that I can get my hands on regarding Spirituality.

Shirley MacLaine, Stuart Wilde, Vianna Stibal, Edgar Cayce, Barbara Hand Clow, and various other writers have been very influential with all the research that I have done over my many years. I have also taken courses that appeal to my curiosity and wonderment.

As I look back and think about my younger years, Shirley MacLaine has always been an inspiration for me. I remember watching one of her movies when I was about 5 years old. She was dancing in the movie, which she did in many of her movies, and I remember that I wanted to be a great dancer like her. She has inspired me in so many ways over the years; the list is long, like the lists of books that she has written, and the movies that she has been in. So, thank you, Shirley, for being such an amazing ray of love and light on this planet.

What If...We Are Not All HERE,

Most of my experiences have been positive in nature. Some have been very scary, especially when I was very young, that have changed my perspective with understanding that things are not always the way you see them. Everything on and around this planet seems to be very real, very strong, and unending; sometimes situations occur that seem to lift the veil for us.

There are parts within this book that are repeated. The reasoning for this is to re-format your sub-conscious and conscious minds to correspond with our super-conscious mind.

So, What If...

HISTORY

'Cause We Are Not All THERE.

What If ...We are not alone here?

I have been blessed with the understanding that we have never been alone on this planet. There have always been other beings on this planet since it was formed. There is documented pottery that has been found in recent years showing dinosaurs and humans working and living together. So, just for a "ha, ha" moment, this makes me think of the cartoon "The Flintstones."

Scientists have confirmed that there are at least 400 Billion planets in our galaxy alone, and that this Universe is approximately 13.8 Billion years old with Mother Earth being approximately 4.6 Billion years old.

So, I must ask...how could anyone possibly think that we are the only life forms that exist anywhere?

Also, is it possible that human life has existed on this planet for Millions of years instead of 10,000 – 15,000 years?

What If...We Are Not All HERE,

What If...You knew the true story of how life began on this planet?

Would you keep it locked up inside of you for years, until the moment was right to get it into print?

Would you think that you are some kind of crazy person having conversations with a Divine Intelligence, our space brothers and sisters, our ancestors, our higher selves, our sub-conscious or conscious minds? Or, put it down to imagination?

There are a lot of things that have happened on this planet for which our scientists have no plausible explanation. They are, and have always been, working on finding solutions, and for the most part, working on finding out the truth. It never ends.

I remember, as a child, I had questions about everything. Most of the time, I looked to the skies for the answers, sometimes I would talk to a family member. As I am sure many of you have, also.

As a child, I had what is usually called "unearthly encounters," what I mean by that is, I would receive telepathic information that would flow through every fiber of my being. Sometimes it would scare me, and other times, everything felt peaceful. This is partly how I came to understand whether I was being truthfully informed, or was misunderstanding a situation.

Wherever it came from, this information very strongly influenced me in this lifetime. The purpose here is to help everyone start asking questions about everything in life, opening your heart and eyes, trusting in your gut, which is attached to your heart, not relying upon others to find your life's questions. Do your own research; the information is out there as well as within you. With all the internet information, as well as programs on TV, Netflix, Gaia TV, or whatever you happen to watch, the information is out there on the World Wide networks.

'Cause We Are Not All THERE.

At the same time, don't always believe what another is telling you, their point of view may be distorted from their experiences. You may hear the whole story from anyone, but yet, only part of the story rings true for you, and that's okay.

Stop allowing others to influence your choices that do not make you happy. Stop living in fear, confusion, chaos, greed, lies, hatred, madness, lack of faith in yourself, lack of self-esteem, lack of anything and everything, etc..

We all need to know who we are, where we came from, where we are going, and what is in store for us. Where or what is our final destination?

Is it to become one with the being of many names (God/Goddess, Creator, Allah, Mohammed, Mother/Father, Divine Intelligence, etc.), on other planets in other solar systems?

Are we here for a dual purpose such as balancing our Ying/Yang, or our God/Goddess perspectives?

Who really knows the answers to these questions?

What If...We Are Not All HERE,

What If….We never needed the saying "History always repeats itself?" When we have finally learned our lessons, acknowledge, and thank the lessons, we then have the opportunity to move forward with ease and grace.

I sometimes imagine that this world is so balanced and in harmony that these visions actually bring tears to my eyes. It has been a very long time in Earth years since this planet has been this way. I know with all my heart that it will again be this way.

I guess the saying "Come Hell or High Water" might need to be applied again in this cycle of the evolution of this planet and all its inhabitants. This has happened a few times in our past, and I sometimes wonder if it will happen again!

'Cause We Are Not All THERE.

What If...King Arthur really did live on this planet?

Where in the British Isle would he have come from?

Was there a man named Merlin?

Was he a magician or maybe a part of the culture called Tuatha Dé Danann (part of the Druids)?

The information that I have uncovered is that of Irish Mythology that says the Tuatha Dé Danann (pronounced: Tu-a-tha Day Dan-ann), Celtic gods, were members of an ancient race who have inhabited Ireland before the historic Irish. It is believed that they were real beings, and have been credited with the possession of magical powers, great wisdom, and were very telepathic. They are also explained as fallen angels whom are neither good nor evil. They are immortal, possess certain superhuman physical attributes, and are immune to all terrestrial diseases, and are resistant to conventional injuries. They are also known as the "Shining Ones."

I have been searching for more information on the Tuatha Dé Danann and know that there have been other researchers involved in this pursuit. I strongly feel that all the teachings that occurred with the Tuatha Dé Danann were done verbally or telepathically; therefore one will never find any written material on them or their lifestyle.

What If...We Are Not All HERE,

What if....We opened ourselves to experience the Divine Intelligence and allowed the flow of telepathic frequencies into our daily lives, how would that change our perspective on things?

What magical powers do we each possess?

How do we bring forth situations and experiences for our greater understanding to learn while improving our earthly selves so that we may reach higher levels of existence, vibrations, or frequencies?

Would meditation or going within oneself have more of an impact into our daily lives with our perspectives and insights with manifesting or bringing forth all that is for our highest and purest good?

'Cause We Are Not All THERE.

What If...Humanity originated in Australia instead anywhere else on this planet?

What would that mean to you?

Would it mean that the color of our skin makes us who we think we are?

It has been said that one of the oldest known civilizations on this planet are the Australian Aboriginals. Their ancestry can be dated back to 60,000 years ago, or possibly more, and it is believed that they were a part of the LeMurian family.

With this being said, how does this change your perspective of what we are taught by our educational systems?

I know with all my heart that there is valuable information out there somewhere that has not been available to researchers. Information will be discovered regarding the original inhabitants of Australia, and I think it will go back possibly millions of our Earth years.

What If…We Are Not All HERE,

What If…The beings that came to reside on this planet came from another galaxy, another solar system, or possibly from one of our own star constellations?

There is a story that you may have heard regarding LeMuria, or Mu as it was usually called. The land that these beings lived on can still be seen, as their megalithic structures now reside on the bottom of the ocean near Japan; and all the smaller islands around the Pacific Ocean that exist today were all a part of this land mass of LeMuria.

These beings from Mu came to this planet, from either another planet in our solar system or possibly another Universe.

From whence they came doesn't really matter. That was many millions of years ago in our Earth time as we know it today. I have seen visions within my third eye showing me what life was like for them on this planet. They were (what we would call magical beings), multi-dimensional beings; they could visualize with a thought a piece of fruit like an apple on the palm of their hand.

They were very tall, fair skinned beings, very peaceful, and they were androgynous (meaning they balanced both the feminine and masculine energy within themselves). I think this is where the so called "garden of Eden" began. They were beings that practiced **The Law of One**, meaning that they were **One** with everything that surrounded them.

Being androgynous means that you have all the body parts of a man and a woman to impregnate yourself if that's what you choose; they would place themselves into a tube of liquid while pregnant until the baby was due to be born. I believe this is a huge part of our ancestral heritage that has been lost for hundreds of thousands of years, maybe even longer than we can speculate.

These beings from Mu were not the first to arrive here, as there were other beings around the now known continent of Africa. These beings would be known to us today as the Anunnaki. Now, as in the

'Cause We Are Not All THERE.

human species (male and female), there were 2 aspects of these beings. Let's call them the Anunnaki and the Illuminati, just to understand the polarities.

The Illuminati were the kind of beings that one would not want to mess with, so-to-speak. They were greedy, out for what they could take, ruled with an iron-fist over others, etc…

Now, on the other side of the coin were the Anunnaki, who for all purposes, were the opposite of the Illuminati, but at the same time, to a certain degree, wanted some control over the DNA sequences that they were formulating. So, while the Illuminati stayed around the area of Africa, the Anunnaki traveled to other spaces on this planet such as Iraq, Iran, Saudi Arabia, Sumeria, etc…

What If...We Are Not All HERE,

What If...The Anunnaki and the Illuminati were the first beings from their world that came to this planet to reap the rewards of the minerals that they needed to sustain their lives and their ancestry?

By the way, their red planet is back in our solar system; I saw it for about 2 weeks around 2015.

What if this planet was not the first planet in our solar system to have life on it?

What if other beings, from other galaxies or star constellations resided on Mars or Venus first, or for that matter, Saturn, before coming to this planet?

Are there other Earth type planets in other galaxies or universes?

What if human life began on Mars or Venus and they were at one time lush and beautiful planets just like our Mother Earth?

What if this planet alone was trillions of years old instead of the billions of years old, that our scientists believe it is?

Carbon dating can only go so far.

'Cause We Are Not All THERE.

What If...The Illuminati were mining on this planet until there was an upheaval from the miners who were living a lifestyle like ours today?

Were they a society of social standing, from upper power to lower power? Did they have a hierarchy system in place?

The information that has been delivered through me has stated that these so-called lower class workers decided at some point that they finally had enough of being controlled, and not being allowed to reap the benefits like the upper echelon beings within their society. These beings, of course, were very intelligent; the greatest fault of the Illuminati was that they were greedy, and they wanted everything that they could take to sustain themselves. It was the elite that would start experimenting on the DNA sequences of creating beings that they could control, and own dominion over. Once they created a species that would do as they were told, and never question their authority, the Illuminati decided to be the first governing beings on this planet, having World domination for only their benefit.

ATLANTIS

This is where our separation from one another, with division, amnesia, dualistic and diversity came in.

Was humanity commanded by the "gods" to take an oath to obey, not ask any questions; not practice anything other than what you are told to practice?

Humans are not worthy of being like the gods that we are, we (the Illuminati) are stronger and more powerful then you feeble minded humans.

Those who worshipped and obeyed these so-called gods would receive all that they wanted which was a false sense of security. These

What If…We Are Not All HERE,

"gods" are all about controlling, manipulation, deception, greed, lies, pain and suffering to others, and brain washing humanity to believe that we have never been as powerful as they are. Is this what is happening with society today?

'Cause We Are Not All THERE.

What if...Native legends and folklore are right when they said that we are now living in the 5th life cycle on Earth?

What do they mean by this?

My interpretation of this information is that human life on this planet has been around for millions of years instead of thousands of years.

I strongly feel that the very first humans created on this planet were living in the area of what we now call Africa and the Middle East.

The 2nd life cycle was called LeMuria or Mu, which was located just off the coast of Japan with all the land mass between Japan, Australia, Hawaii, Easter Island, and all the Islands in between.

The 3rd life cycle was called Atlantis, which was located between America (USA) and Europe. There are a lot of different theories regarding where Atlantis was actually located. I think there are many possibilities and Edgar Cayce knew where it was. He had stated that the road to Atlantis is off the coast of Bimini. Some theorize that the landmass sank into the ocean, while others think that the land mass flew up and out of the water and left the Earth. So, I wonder, how vast in size was Atlantis, and how many pieces of that land mass broke apart before its final demise?

The 4th life cycle was when most of Egypt, Sumeria, Asia, Meso America, and surrounding cultures saw travelers who said they were from LeMuria and Atlantis. It has been documented in hieroglyphs that beings from other Solar Systems also worked with the peoples of those areas for a new evolution of humankind. This process took hundreds of thousands of Earth years to accomplish with educating, demonstrating, and teaching others.

The 5th life cycle is the time line that we are in right now. There are many scientists in many fields who say that the past 10,000 years or so is the only time in Earth's history that humans have evolved. This

What If...We Are Not All HERE,

information is incorrect and they are now finding evidence that they need to re-configure. Carbon dating will never be an exact science, but can give an approximate time line.

'Cause We Are Not All THERE.

What If...We all were created with 12 strong strands of DNA, and the Higher Atlantean beings or other kinds of beings decided to reduce our strands to keep control of the population?

Are these beings what we call the World Management Team, also known as the Anunnaki/Illuminate?

Why did we allow this to happen?

Did we have a say in this matter?

How can we change things right now?

Do you want to change things?

If your answer is YES, then we all need to raise our consciousness and frequencies, and allow the programming aspect of who we think we are to be more loving, respectful, and grateful of all we receive and all we can give to ourselves and others.

Are you happy to be a drone, a zombie, ignoring what's happening all over the world?

Humans are killing other humans as well as animals for profit instead of sustainability. Are we really being guided to slaughter cows by the millions every day to feed the populations?

What about the countries where humans are starving to death, literally?

Why are our government officials allowing this?

What is really going on here?

I for one would like to hear the truth and understand why.

As far as I see it, everything is about having profit, power, placing fear, greed, etc...

What If...We Are Not All HERE,

Quote from the Bible: *"The Love of Money is the root of all Evil"*; I believe that the root of all evil is one's desire for power. The Catholic churches have always been about profit. Look at the Vatican for instance, with all the marble, tapestries, etc... Money, greed, wealth, taxes, etc. are how they are able to build the fortresses that they call the Vatican. Even now, they are still receiving money for the upkeep of not only the Vatican, but all other churches, with all religions around the world. Even the Mormons are allowed to take 15% of their parishioner's monthly income.

How fair is that?

Why are they allowed to do so?

Is it because the people that attend any church must pay to pray?

Why has there been a monetary value put on our "Souls" and our Spiritual well being and growth?

'Cause We Are Not All THERE.

W hat If...Our seemingly fragile physical bodies were created and designed to be strong and healthy while maintaining balance with our emotional, mental, physical and spiritual health for at least hundreds if not for thousands of years?

There is information that I came across many years ago that is being investigated now regarding our distant past history; various researchers including William Henry, Graham Hancock, Erich von Däniken, Freddy Silva and many others, have found documented proof that there have been many civilizations around this planet where humans have lived for thousands of years. (Some have been thought of as living for 30,000 years).

With that being said, how can the scientific communities still ignore the fact that humans have been on this planet for possibly millions of years instead of only 12,000 years?

What If...We Are Not All HERE,

What If....You looked at and studied the Mayan Calendar, what would you find?

Author Barbara Hand Clow has written some very informative books on this subject of Native cultures and the Mayan civilizations of the distant past. She has stated that the Mayan Calendar has an evolutionary cycle for 50,000 years, and according to her research, there have been many cycles. How did the ancient Mayan know this information, and where did it come from?

According to our scientific community, this planet is billions of years old, so why wouldn't humans be able to exist on this planet long before 12,000 years on our time table?

Why does our history only seem to start after the last ice age which is called the Younger Dryas?

What happened before that time-line in our Earth's history?

'Cause We Are Not All THERE.

What If...Our space brothers and sisters never interfered with the evolutionary process on this planet?

Or came to visit us and educate us on energy, mathematics, astrology, astronomy, etc..?

Where do you think we would be on the Evolutionary scale for humanity?

Would we or could we still be in what is called the Neolithic period of mankind?

In our distant past, meaning hundreds of thousands of years ago, were our ancestors more spiritually advanced then we are today?

When in our history did the Giants appear?

When was the time that the feminine energies ruled this planet, and was their fall from grace created by the imbalance of only feminine energy while ignoring the masculine energy that is required to balance oneself?

Why have there been giant skeletons unearthed, thrown out to the media, and then classified as TOP SECRET?

Why was the Smithson family from England, who started the Smithsonian Museum in the United States or the Universities in England, allowed to hide important information from the public that would possibly help with our evolution here?

What If...We Are Not All HERE,

What If...All the Great Pyramids around our planet were built hundreds of thousands of years ago, before the end of the last Ice Age?

What are the possibilities of the Pyramids being built millions of years ago?

Just because archeologists discovered a wooden ship next to the Great Pyramid in Giza, does not mean that this ship was buried there right after the pyramids were built. All that it illustrates to me is that the people were very proud of the fact that they were a society that sailed the seas and traded goods with other civilizations.

Where the Pyramids created as power stations?

Where they connected to all the other pyramids around this planet as a power grid, not only for light but for spiritual practices and initiations to the higher dimensions or densities?

Are the Pyramids portals turning into wormholes for traveling on and off this planet?

'Cause We Are Not All THERE.

What If...All the archeologists on this planet who are working on deciphering information from ancient civilizations are so close to truly understanding what the hieroglyphs, pictographs, and writings are really all about?

I understand that the only reason why many scientists are not following through with the information that they have discovered is based on criticism and ridicule from their colleagues, which could lead to them losing their tenure.

We have books that have been written with someone's interpretation of a variety of circumstances; does that mean that their findings are the truth?

Have they interpreted this information correctly?

Over the many millions of years that humans have resided on this planet, there have been many languages. Take a look at the English language for instance. Only 200 - 300 years ago, the English language was far removed from what it is today. All languages, much like the forms of everything on, in, and around this planet, evolve and change.

What If...We Are Not All HERE,

What If...The darker or shadow energies in and around this planet really want to take over this entire Universe?

There are millions of possibilities and probabilities that occur every moment, whether we are asleep or in our waking lives.

Did the life forms that we call the Dark energies already destroy their system where they first originated?

From what I understand, the answer is a very strong YES. As I see it, they are trying it again, and maybe, just maybe things will turn out for them.

If we all stand strong together instead of being SHEEPLE like they want us to be, there is nothing that can or will stand in our way. The power of the people is where we need to be, standing side by side in harmony, peace, and love. The words "Together at Last" come to mind.

Have some of our scientists sold their souls to the darker energies on this planet?

Is this where all these AI formats and 5G are coming from?

Do they really think they will fix everything on this planet with robots?

Why don't some scientists believe that humans have a soul or spirit?

Do they all need to experience "Near Death" to really understand what's happening and the destruction of our future?

Are they just being puppets for the puppet masters out of fear?

What is the truth behind everything that is happening since the Harmonic convergence in 1987?

'Cause We Are Not All THERE.

Unfortunately, it's not just the scientists who are being brainwashed, it's also some of the elite or wealthy that are a part of the World Management Team; we have actors, actresses, musicians, and the like deceiving the population.

There are many Spiritual Warriors on this planet. We all need to help one another get to where we need to be on the evolutionary ladder. So, open your ears and hearts, really listen to what others are saying, watch their body language, really look into their eyes; is there life in those eyes, or are they dazed and confused?

The other day, while I was at work I was reading an article that stated that Digital IDs are linked to a social credit score. There is now a programmable digital currency and it's based on the UN (United Nations) agenda for the next decade to have this mandatory digital ID and control for the billionaire elites called "Controligarchs" according to Seamus Bruner, who is an author, investigative journalist and the Director of Research at the Government Accountability Institute.

Seamus Burner's new book is called "Controligarchs: Exposing the Billionaire Class, their Secret Deals, and the Globalist Plot to Dominate Your Life." In this book he exposes the influence of billionaires like Bill Gates, Mark Zuckerberg, and BlackRock, just to name a few, who prefer to have control over our lives when it comes to vaccines, media, agriculture, and various other sectors of our lives.

So in short, some of these people want to control everyone's life, all the while, using their power and influences on the governments to seize control over everything. They want digital currencies, ID's, and social credit scores. In this way, they can make sure that humanity will always be tracked. They want to know how much money you have, where you are spending it, when you are spending it, and if they think that you are spending too much money, they will have access to lowering your social credit score, and if you don't follow their specific "RULES" you will then be at risk of being banned or have your finances frozen.

What If...We Are Not All HERE,

Have these humans sold their Souls?

For what - more power, more money?

This is outrageous. If these changes were to happen, and I am praying very hard that they don't happen, we will no longer have any privacy.

Does anyone on this planet really want to be crushed and forced to depend entirely on a centralized system that controls everything that you work for, including your own sanity?

I for one choose to expand my awareness and non-compliance to this kind of behaviour. We really need to stand together for our own peace of mind, to be the sovereign beings that we have always been; and work together in co-operation instead of competition, for a common goal that includes everyone.

'Cause We Are Not All THERE.

What If ...The Harmonic Convergence in 1987 was about raising our energetic levels of consciousness as well as shifting some of our chakras back to their original states?

From the understandings that I have received, when Atlantis finally broke apart and sank into the (Atlantic) ocean, there was a catastrophic malfunction with the Earth energy grids and the ley lines around this planet.

Was it at this time in our distant past that our chakras were changed?

I was informed in my youth that originally we were all created with at least 12 strands of DNA, possibly more. Our Heart chakra was Red, our Base chakra was Blue, and our Naval chakra was Green. At some point, our chakras were changed.

Why? What was the purpose of these chakra changes?

With our chakras placed back into their original positions, they represent the Christ Consciousness Energy, and help humanity stay grounded to the Earth in a loving, healing manner for all.

When the colours were changed from the Heart, Base and Naval chakras (now, Green for the Heart, Orange for the Naval, and Red for the Base) it changed the dynamic structure of our processing spectrums. With the Base now being Red, this would mean that the population of beings on this planet would grow astronomically. At the same time, still be a little grounded to the Earth energies, and no longer understanding who we truly are. A little amnesia, or a lot, either way, the change happened. Eventually, all things will begin to heal and revert back to their original state of being.

Now, in this 21st century, we also received another change to all the energy grids on this planet as well as within each and every being on this planet, and that was the Mayan Calendar (also called the T'zolkin

What If...We Are Not All HERE,

Calendar) dated for 12/12/2012. The energy that was occurring was one of restructure for humanity, the evolutionary process of Mother Earth and cementing all the changes that needed of occur for the greater good for all.

So now I must ask, with all the different healing modalities that are being practiced on a moment by moment basis, why are teachers and/or instructors not being informed about these chakra changes?

The traditional 7 colors of the rainbow charkas:

Base Chakra: Red – Material or Physical Energy – Earth Element

Navel Chakra: Orange – Sexual Energy – Fire Element

Solar Plexus: Yellow – Power – Fire Element

Heart Chakra: Green – Love – Water Element

Throat Chakra: Blue – Expression – Air Element

Third Eye Chakra: Indigo – Cosmic Intelligence – Air Element

Crown Chakra: Violet or White – Divinity – Quintessence – God Consciousness

Since the Harmonic Convergence as well as the Mayan Calendar happening in the 20th century, all our chakras have exchanged colours, and we can now add in the Thymus chakra which is Aquamarine in colour. This chakra takes care of our immune system and our metabolism. It has a crystalline connection to the Divine with the Divine Heart.

There are many teachers still going by the 7 chakra system that they themselves have been instructed to utilize, but now times have changed. I have always believed that we were created with more then just 7 chakras, just like our DNA. In total, there are at least 33 or more chakras that each being is surrounded by in higher levels of beingness and consciousness.

'Cause We Are Not All THERE.

Our new 13 Chakra System

Root Chakra – Located around 1 foot below your feet into Mother Earth/the Goddess/Gaia.

These roots flow down to the Crystalline Heart of this planet, just like the roots from the flora.

Colour is Dark Brown (This is the colour that came to me).

Feet Chakra – Located on the bottom of your feet, this is your direct physical connection that helps to anchor and ground you to Mother Earth/Sophia/Gaia.

Colour is Brown (This is the colour that came to me).

Knee Chakra – Located at the front and back of our Knee's, allowing the physical body flexibility emotionally, mentally, physically, and spiritually.

Colour is Indian Red (This is the colour that came to me).

Basic/Sex Chakra – Located at the base of your Spine, both in the front and the back of your body in the pubic area.

This is the center for physical creativity and action.

Colour is Sapphire Blue.

What If...We Are Not All HERE,

Naval Chakra – Located at the Naval in the front of the body.

This is your true brain, trusting your "gut instincts."

Colour is Emerald Green.

Meng Mein Chakra – Located at the back of your Naval.

This chakra works on regulating your kidneys and adrenal glands, and helps to control blood pressure.

Colour is Emerald Green.

Spleen/Solar-Plexus Charka – Located in the front of the Solar-Plexus, positioned between your ribs. The back of the Solar-Plexus is located behind the Spleen.

This chakra influences the other chakras of all our lower emotions like anger, fear, worry, anxiety, etc... This is also where your "I" as in "I want this," or "I want that" is located.

Colour is Golden Yellow.

Heart Chakra – Located in the center of your chest and is located in the front and back of our body.

This is where higher emotions like peace, joy, compassion, kindness, patience, etc. are located.

Colour is Red.

'Cause We Are Not All THERE.

Thymus Chakra – Located in the upper chest at the base of your neck.

This is your body's center that is comprised of the large lymphoid tissue that functions the development of our immune system. It is the link between our Heart and physical body.

Colour is Aquamarine.

Throat Chakra – Located in the center of your throat.

This is the center for higher creativity. When the Throat and Basic chakras are combined together, they create a strong sexual drive in humans.

Colour is Electric Blue.

Third-Eye Chakra – Located in the center of your Eyebrows. This chakra is also called the Ajna Chakra, or the All Seeing Eye (of Horus).

This is where your higher abstract mind for understanding concepts and principles are, which help enhance our intensions and willpower.

Colour is Violet.

Crown Chakra – Located at the top of your head.

This is where we receive higher cosmic consciousness, higher intuition. This is the center of Soul Realization or Illumination. This is where Divine Love, Universal Love, Spiritual energy, or the Soul can enter the physical body.

Colour is White.

What If...We Are Not All HERE,

Higher-Self Chakra – Located around 1 foot above your Crown chakra.

This is where we start our Spiritual Ascension with anchoring our Higher Consciousness realms with our "I AM" presence, or your "God/Goddess" self. This is coming together as One with All That Is with the Universal and Collective Consciousness with our physical body.

Colour is Golden.

As far as I see it, we all have a total of 13 chakras that all consist of the Earth Elements at our disposal to utilize and work with. We also have all the meridians (see a Chinese Medicine chart) within our human form and the Earth energy grids.

Everything is energy. Everything always flows and grows. Now is the time for humanity to start healing Oneself before we can truly heal another. Each and every being on this planet is here to work on the core level of self. By acknowledging, taking full and complete responsibility for yourself, understanding who you truly are (especially all our monsters in the closet), by facing your situations in all moments without judgement, criticism, self- loathing or lack of worth. It is hard work, especially when you question your truths, your belief patterns, and all the programming that has been downloaded through you and to you throughout your many lifetimes. This is hard work that we all are here to accomplish in this lifetime. I can only speak for myself and my experiences when I say "Nobody ever said that life was meant to be easy….I promise that your life will be worth the roller coaster ride."

'Cause We Are Not All THERE.

W hat If...All these underground tunnel systems through our planet were created millions of years before our time now, tunnels that were created to save humanity during strong environmental changes like the great flood and Ice Ages that have occurred on this planet?

Research shows that the human species have existed for at least 1.9 million years.

It has also been stated that Hominids existed on this planet somewhere between 6 million years ago and ended approximately 5.3 million years ago.

What really happened and why?

Was this a time when our beloved planet was coming into her 1st or 2nd change of life for herself?

Was this around the time humans were learning to build tunnel and cave systems?

When did our space brothers and sisters first come to this planet?

SPIRITUALITY

'Cause We Are Not All THERE.

What If….We were all taught from the beginning of this incarnation into our physical bodies, that we are truly never alone?

Of course we have all our family members. Do you know that each and every one of us has what have been called 'Guardian Angels' that incarnate along with us in this lifetime?

We have at our disposal, Ascended Masters, Arch Angels, our Spirit Guides, Animal Guides, our Ancestors, our Higher Selves, Over-Souls, and our I Am Presence along with the entire Divine Intelligence which are all very happy to help and assist us at any moment.

All we need to do is ask for their assistance. When we sit quietly, as in meditation, quieting our minds from racing down a rabbit hole, and open ourselves up to all the possibilities and probabilities, wonderful things occur for us.

When we tune in, like fine tuning a radio station, we allow ourselves to become the antenna for more spiritual understandings. There is so much help available to us, and all we need to do is just be. Be in the moment. Be the divine sovereign being that you are. We may not get the answers to our questions the way we formulate them to come, but we will always get an answer the best way possible.

Let's say you are having issues with a loved one. Find a quiet space where you will not be disturbed. You can lie down, or sit cross legged (lotus position), focus on your breath. Breathe in for the count of 4, hold for 2, and then breathe out for 4. Keep focusing on the breath until the mind calms down.

You can say a prayer, chant a mantra, whatever you feel comfortable with, and ask for the guidance that you are seeking. The answer may come to you immediately or may take some time. Let go of any and all expectations.

What If...We Are Not All HERE,

Answers always come differently; they happen when you may be walking or jogging; they may come from animals or birds. They may even come through when you are having a conversation with another. All you are required to do is to be yourself without expectations or demands. Allow all the energies that are needed and necessary to flow.

'Cause We Are Not All THERE.

What If...As we are birthed into this incarnation, society held the values of the Spiritual connections to All-That-Is?

What happened in our distant past that societies have seemingly forgotten about these virtues?

What would our world be like if we all were encouraged from a tender age to enhance our spiritual gifts and talents that we have all been inherently blessed with?

Fine tuning some of our abilities will help bring through stronger energies and frequencies for not only this school room, Mother Earth, but for the entire Universe and Cosmos.

There are 8 different abilities that we posses along with all our senses. They are as follows:

Clair-Voyance: *Clear-seeing* – The ability to receive information through visions. This information comes from one's Crown chakra down to one's Third Eye chakra.

Clair-Cognizance: *Clear-knowing* – The ability of intuitively knowing the information is coming from the Divine Source, Spirit Guides, your High Self, etc...

Clair-Audience: *Clear-hearing* – The ability to hear sounds from other realms. Such as 'ringing in your ears' and hearing voices.

Clair-Salience: *Clear-smelling* – The ability to smell odors, like the sweet smell of some perfumes from a loved one that has passed away.

Clair-Gustance: *Clear-tasting* – The ability to taste without indulging in anything like pastry from a baker that is no longer in the physical realm.

Clair-Tangency: *Clear-touch* – The ability to touch or hold onto an object and receive clear intuitive information regarding that person's life.

Clair-Sentience: *Clear-feeling* – The ability to receive information through feeling a person's body that has passed away.

Clair-Empathy: *Clear-emotions* – The ability to physically experience thoughts, pain/hurts, and attitudes from people, places, or animals.

'Cause We Are Not All THERE.

What If...There was no such thing as being prejudiced of someone or something, or even being racist regarding someone's skin color, religion, belief system, or anything else for that matter?

What would this World be like if at least ¼ of the population searched deep within oneself by going to the very Heart of the matter to understand where their programming came from?

Would you choose to change your perspective?

What would be the probability of expanding your awareness and motivation to change your mindset?

Could you see yourself as part of the solution or would you choose to be or stay the problem?

What's in store for the human population?

Would you choose to come together as one, or would you choose to be separate from others?

What If...We Are Not All HERE,

What If...Your race, creed, religion, beliefs, your sexual preferences, etc.., didn't matter to anyone but you?

How long has this thought behaviour been acceptable on this planet?

Why is this acceptable behaviour?

What makes one person think that they are better than someone else?

Is it their upbringing, education, religion, mental programming, or lack thereof?

Why do we do the things that we do?

Are we bringing past-life experiences forward?

Do you know or understand that you have a blueprint for your adventure here?

A Spiritual teacher, Rose Sangregorio, from Calgary, Alberta, Canada has written in her book "Journey to Self-Enlightenment":

> *"Each soul carries with it an energy matrix of light, which is part of the etheric body (energy that surrounds the physical body). This matrix of light carries all the information for the lifetime the soul is living on earth regarding past, present, and future lives. It also carries the information for karmic learnings and lessons, as well as the gifts and talents the soul carries. This is also energetically connected to the higher-self. This is called the silver cord."*

Through my research, I have discovered that each and every person on this planet has lived many lives, and according to some theorists anywhere up to 250 past lives or more, either on this planet or other planets, possibly in other galaxies and universes.

'Cause We Are Not All THERE.

What If...We are all here for a reason, a purpose?

What would that be?

How was your childhood, and that of your parents, aunts and uncles, grandparents, friends, cousins, etc..?

Did anyone make an important impact on your life that has helped you or discouraged you to be who you are today?

I am so grateful to have had some very influential people around me while I was a youth. My Great Grandpa was a very loving, caring, and compassionate person who would talk to me about energies that were all around me and how I could play with them when I was alone. He was an amazingly gifted person in so many ways. He passed away December 27th shortly after I turned 4 years old. I recall hearing stories about him from my mom and my grandma (her father). When I was 13 years old, I was staying at my Grandma's place for the weekend. My uncle was away with Sea Cadets, so I got to stay in his room. I loved that room because my uncle had psychedelic wallpaper.

One night while I was sound asleep, I found myself waking up and looking into the hallway. The moon was full and was shining through the hallway window, all of a sudden, there seemed to be a mist in the hallway. I heard some wet squeaky shoe walking on the carpet and saw a shadow figure in the doorway. I remember feeling like I couldn't move or scream for my grandma, then all of a sudden, this sweet voice came into my thoughts and said "I am your Great Grandpa, I have come to see you and to speak with you about your life. I won't be able to stay long as I have a great deal of work to do on the other side." I was no longer scared, I felt a warm glow as he talked to me and gave me information. Then he said "I am so sorry that I can not come back to see you again, but when it's your time to cross-over, I will be there with loving arms to embrace you."

What If...We Are Not All HERE,

What If ...We believe that our reality (our waking world) is nothing but a dream world, and our dream world (sleep time) is our true reality?

What constitutes something as real or a dream?

What about lucid dream time, when we are in the state of partially awake and partially asleep?

Are they all one of the same, or are they slightly different?

It has been theorized that everything on and of this planet is an illusion. What we see as walls, furniture, all material items that you can think of are all particles of energy coming together to help us perceive them as solid.

Just because a human can use their 5 senses on what we believe to be real, is it really real, or is it a dream?

It has been stated by many philosophers throughout our history that our 5 senses are all self-identifiers with our body and not with our consciousness. Our Self-Identity is our perceptions with our experiences. So, what we believe, we perceive. What we perceive, we experience. If you believe that you can not achieve a goal or manifest a possibility, then it will not happen, but if you believe that you can achieve a goal or manifest a possibility, you will.

The Mystic/Alchemist called Paracelsus stated that there are the 3 Edicts and they are:

> 1 – **Imagination** – *Picture what you want to manifest into your reality, and know with all your heart that it will manifest.*
>
> 2 – **Faith** – *Knowing and trusting in your ability to manifest all that is for your highest and greatest good without any doubts.*

'Cause We Are Not All THERE.

*3 – **Will** – Having the Will to stay on course with what you have chosen to manifest/create.*

What is the difference between Belief and Faith?

Belief is when you think things may or may not happen, and having doubts with any given situation.

Faith is about knowing and trusting (your gut instincts) oneself regardless of the outcome; everything happens for a reason, for our greater knowledge and understanding.

Does our consciousness and/or sub-consciousness play a role in our life experiences by helping us to understand what is really happening in our lives, and if so, to what extent?

What is the difference between our consciousness and our awareness?

As Jerry Wills (Healer) describes the differences, I quote:

"Consciousness is like a light that hits the wall and your conscious says "that's a light hitting the wall."

Our Awareness is looking at the wall and understanding what we are seeing on the wall. The more aware that you are, the more aware you can become. Awareness is what gives you the feedback that allows you to ask the question "Why?""

For example: I had the feeling that I needed to pay attention before this situation happened, so why did I ignore myself?

I heard people say "I am a realist," what does that mean?

When I have asked them what they think it means, they comment: "when I can see it, feel it, touch it, taste it, or hear it, I know and have proof that it's real."

What If…We Are Not All HERE,

So then I ask "what about love?" Do you love your family, mate, or your friends?" They say "Yes."

Then I say "okay, can you prove to me that you love others?"

I then usually have people walk away from me, or they stop talking to me, which I find quite funny. Or they say "no I can not prove it, I just know it."

I would say that that is not being a realist; it's all about our perspectives and understandings that are occurring because we have the ability to utilize our 5 senses, and/or our so called, God given talents.

It has been stated by many scientific theorists that we all use a very small percentage of our brain capacity. Is this why we seem to have limited perspectives and perceptions on any given situation?

How can we all expand our minds, our thoughts, or our brains to "wake-up" and truly discover what is real or a dream?

Does our physical state (waking) or the dream state have anything to do with our heart energy, or does that energy come from our Over Soul/Higher Self/I Am Presence?

'Cause We Are Not All THERE.

What If...The day that you die or cross-over into the Spirit form, you have a review of all the situations that occurred in this lifetime?

Does your spirit come back on the same date that you exited?

Do you know why you came here to this 3rd dimensional planet called Mother Earth?

What lessons are you here to learn and understand and gain additional wisdom from?

Would it be about self-forgiveness?

Would it be about Self-empowerment?

Would it be about becoming one with All That Is, the Divine Intelligence (Creator, God/Goddess, Allah, Yahweh, the being that goes by many names)?

What If...We Are Not All HERE,

What If ...You were informed by an Intuitive/Psychic reader that this will be your last incarnation on this Earth plane?

Would you get excited about not coming back to this planet?

Would you ask any questions as to where your next incarnation will be?

Would you say, "awesome," I don't have to come back to this schoolroom planet of hard knocks anymore. Would you accept that to be your reality, and that is that?

I have come across a few people who have stated that they were informed that this is their last time here. They all seemed so very happy and joyful about this statement that they had a hard time calming down and thinking rationally.

I recall asking them "so, are you moving forward on your path to higher dimensions from Mother Earth, or are you going onto other Earth type planets that are of lower dimensions/frequencies and realities?"

When I have asked my questions, people seem to respond with a confused look on their faces and tell me that they didn't think of asking any questions, they were just happy to hear the so-called good news. But is it really good news?

Why have we all been programmed to resist asking any in-depth questions?

I understand that in our past (whether in this lifetime or other lifetimes), we have all been criticized, made fun of, tortured, beaten, enslaved, or cast out of our societies for questioning and asking for greater understanding, knowledge, and clarity of any circumstance, but things are not so strict and unrelenting in the 21st century with most societies on this planet. We are all slowly waking-up, and moving forward with either a lot of resistance or a little resistance. Either way, there is still resistance that needs to be embraced and forgiven.

'Cause We Are Not All THERE.

Why are we still placing FEAR at the forefront of all our lives (past, present, and our future) instead of confronting it?

Are we here to acknowledge the fear that is at this moment, by asking for forgiveness of oneself as well as others and embracing that fear with loving kindness in order to move forward in our evolution of spiritual growth and oneness?

The scientific community has stated for many years that there are many Earth type planets in our galaxy that sustain life in all forms. So, what are the possibilities and probabilities that the frequencies/energies of these other Earth type planets are higher or lower, and how will they affect our so-called reality?

Will our outlook on these Earth type planets be more harmonious, or are they more dangerous?

If you are looking for more information regarding these other worlds, you can go to the Gaia Network and look for Cosmic Disclosure with David Wilcox and Emery Smith who interview the people who have been involved for many years in the various Secret Space Programs. These interviewee's are in Special-Forces and all have similar stories with the different programs that are happening with the world's military structures.

What If...We Are Not All HERE,

What If ...We all understood that our physical bodies worked with their own Divine Intelligence?

What I mean by this is what if all the aches and pains that we feel within our bodies are providing us with the information of what we are thinking and/or feeling on a sub-conscious level?

Let me provide you with an example: What if you're lower back or your sciatic nerve was feeling discomfort, and became irritating?

Would you want to take something to relieve the pain immediately or would you go within to discover what or who is a pain in your butt/ass?

What will you discover about this situation, and why did you create this pain or imbalance?

Where did this dis-comfort come from, did you create this mentally, emotionally, physically, or spiritually?

What is the gemstone or bottom-line (no pun intended) behind this experience?

What perspective would you create to relieve your body of this pain and discomfort?

Are you ready and willing to go as deep as possible, taking full responsibility for your thoughts, words, deeds, and actions?

You are the creator and co-creator of all your own experiences', everyone else is merely a reflection of your beingness. No matter what you are experiencing, everything works from your perspective, knowledge, and awareness either from your conscious or your sub-conscious levels. So, what will you do to regain balance within as well as without your beingness?

'Cause We Are Not All THERE.

What If...You had the opportunity to ask at least one heart-felt question everyday for the rest of your life, what do you think would happen?

Where would you be?

Who would you tell, or would you keep the information all to yourself?

There are millions of possibilities and probabilities in this life, as well as in the entire history of this planet.

Why?

Is it because of change?

Change happens every moment of our lives; this is the only constant that exists that we know of. What you thought a moment ago is now gone, and another thought has come into your mind.

The history and mystery of our Universe along with the Earth has been vast for millions if not billions of our years. When and where did it all begin?

Is this what we are calling legends, myths, fairytales, mysteries of the unknown, etc..?

Whatever it is that you choose to call all these stories, somewhere, there will always be some form of the truth from the story teller; and also misinterpretations. As any story goes, there will always be a person's perspective on any given situation, their interpretation of what really happened or what may have possibly happened.

Have you ever been in a classroom, where one person whispers a story to someone and they in turn whisper the story to the next person, then on and on?

What If...We Are Not All HERE,

Usually, by the time the story is relayed to the 3rd or 4th person, the story is all messed up. When the story reaches the last person, they probably got a few ands & buts correct, and that is about it. That would explain why we can not find much documentation from our ancient ancestors; the majority of their experiences were dictated through the spoken word instead of being written down on some form of papyrus or paper. Besides that fact, the variety of languages that there are in this day and age is completely different from what was.

'Cause We Are Not All THERE.

What If...We all had the opportunity to speak to beings from another World or solar system?

How would the conversation go?

Would everything be done telepathically, verbally, through sign-language, vibrations of energy, or, frequencies?

What would you want to talk about?

Where do they come from?

How long did it take them to get to our planet?

Did they go through a worm-hole and if so, how did they know where the worm-hole was?

What kind of technology needs to be acquired in order to go through a worm-hole?

I can speculate that after I got over the initial shock of being in their company, I would be asking more questions than I have documented in this book.

What If...We Are Not All HERE,

What If...There was an Alien Mother Ship behind Saturn that was watching us, controlling us, like little pawns in their machines, or what some have called "The Matrix" (just like the movie) and are they having a strong influence on everything that happens on this planet?

We are now in a day and age where we have the opportunity to think, and research beyond our Universe. So, it makes me wonder, how could we possibly be the only life-forms with millions upon millions of galaxies out there?

Now, I understand that there is a Divine Intelligence or a Creator of All That Is, and there have always been questions on my mind: Where and how did this being create itself?

When did it all begin?

Can we create something out of nothingness?

As legends and stories have been told, there are many tribes of people in this world that have handed down stories of beings from other places, that came here to teach our ancestors how to communicate amongst themselves, build structures, mathematics, that taught them about the solar system, and so much more. Even in the 20th century there are tribes that have no written language, only word of mouth. So, this begs the question: how far back in the history of this planet does this information go?

Does it go back more than a few thousand of years, or does this all go back millions, and perhaps, many billions of years in human history?

My personal thoughts are that all the communicated history goes back many, many millions of years.

'Cause We Are Not All THERE.

What If...Our current life is really like the Matrix?

Could life really be like playing a game on Nintendo or any other computer game?

Are there beings using us as their pawns, running experiments, or even worse?

Is this how they program us and control our every move, thought, and action?

Could this be why computer systems, including street cameras, and vehicles have chips in them?

In recent years it has been reported that Elon Musk has designed a computer chip that is implanted into the brains of injured people. This chip was made available to assist the injured body with walking, talking, running, or any other serious injury that has occurred. I feel that this kind of technology is very beneficial for humanity, as long as it is used for the greater good for all instead of control.

It has been stated that we live in a Free Will Universe. As I now see things, our Free Will is being taken away from all humans, and the order of the day seems to be Control.

We were never meant to be controlled, we are all sovereign beings, our soul has chosen to be here for a physical experience, and to rise above the lessons that we have all come to understand.

What If...We Are Not All HERE,

What If...We all knew and understood everything about the creation of life, the planets, the galaxies, the entire universes, the entire cosmos, when we were born into this world?

I was once informed by a Spiritual Medium of her philosophy of life; she said:

> *"From the time we are born until we are 10 years old,*
> *Our Families do our head in."*
> *"From the time we are 11years old until we are 20 years old,*
> *The Educational systems do our head in."*
> *"From the time we are 21 years old until we are 30 years old,*
> *Our Friends do our head in."*
> *"From the time we are 31 years old until we are 40 years old,*
> *Society does our head in."*
> *"From the time we are 41 years old until we are 50 years old,*
> *We do our head in."*
> *"From 51 years old and onwards, we finally start to get it."*

This amazing being told me this information over 20 years ago. I am doing my best to remember exactly her words. My point is she was so correct with her statement.

'Cause We Are Not All THERE.

What If...You could walk in someone else's shoes for at least 24 to 48 hours?

Would you choose a personal acquaintance, or someone famous, whether they are dead or alive?

What do you think you will experience?

How would this change your life?

What If...We Are Not All HERE,

What If...Forest Gump's momma was right when she said "Life was like a box of chocolates, you never know what's inside"?

What would you change about yourself?

What would enhance your life?

Would you prefer another person's life, or would you appreciate your life more then you do now?

'Cause We Are Not All THERE.

What If...All our lives were interchangeable?

What if all the humans on this planet right now, are really only one Source having billions of experiences at the same time?

Throughout my research and my quest for greater understandings, knowledge, and wisdom, the following words have been ingrained within my heart:

We all come from one Source,

We will all go back to that one Source.

We are the Source that resides within.

As we go within ourselves,

Our Will power will find the truth.

What If...We Are Not All HERE,

What If...Tolerance was one of the most important lessons of our lives to learn and understand?

The Dalai Llama states:

"The person who has a tremendous reserve of patience

and tolerance has a certain degree

of tranquility and calmness in his or her life.

Such a person is not only happy and more

emotionally grounded,

but also seems to be physically healthier

and experiences less illness.

This person possesses a strong will, has a good appetite,

and can sleep with a clear conscience."

Is this the kind of person you are striving to be?

What are your goals to achieve in this lifetime?

What would this planet be like if we taught all our babies to practice "Tolerance"?

'Cause We Are Not All THERE.

What If…We were all created to have the same skin tone, the same thoughts, and the same outlook on life itself?

Or have the same belief systems?

Would there be any need for racism, bigotry, deceit, propaganda?

Would we live freely without any fear or wars or domination?

What If...We Are Not All HERE,

What If...Every human on this planet understood, and deeply believed with every fiber of their being that we are ON this planet Earth, and not OF this planet, meaning that we were all created somewhere other than this planet?

There are some humans who have opened their consciousness levels to receive messages, and document channeled information from our brothers and sisters from systems like Lyra, Pleiades, Orion, etc...

Are these channelings a demonstration to the rest of humanity to see and hear what we are all capable of accomplishing when we are open to focus on our breath, relax, and let go of any or all expectations?

The proof is everywhere, all we need to do is open our eyes and our hearts to truly understand the amazing creations that are on this planet, such as the Great Pyramids, Machu Picchu, and many other wonders of the old world. There are new discoveries all the time; I am positive that where we are with discovering older structures is just the beginning of some amazing creation stories.

'Cause We Are Not All THERE.

What If...We all retained the truth of "All That Is," "All That Ever Was," and "All That Ever Will Be"?

What would this mean for you?

When we are birthed onto this planet, do we hold those frequencies and vibrations?

Why are some humans taught to be afraid of spirit beings?

What is the purpose of being in the dark before we see the light?

What If...We Are Not All HERE,

What If...Every human on this planet saw others as their brothers and sisters and treated them with kindness and love?

What would happen?

Would we need any form of Governmental Justice?

Would we need any form of Religious Power over us?

Would we need any form of negative influence at all?

What if we all created Peace in all our moments?

The Dalai Lama States:

"We can not achieve World Peace

without first achieving

Peace within ourselves...Inner Peace.

In an atmosphere of

Hatred, Anger, Competition and Violence,

NO lasting Peace can be achieved.

These Negative and Destructive

forces must be overcome by

Compassion, Love and Altruism,

which are the essential teachings of

The BUDDHA."

'Cause We Are Not All THERE.

What If...We practiced GRATITUDE for 1 day or 1 week, or every day for the rest of our lives?

Would we actually be on a planet that is creating Peace, with no need for fighting or wars?

Would we all be able to allow others to have their own opinions and perspectives on their surroundings?

Would there be less struggle and strife in daily lives?

When and why was humanity told that we need to constantly strive for money and power?

Was it so that we could all be like the gods that restrict us?

What would happen to this World and our Universe if we all started going within and seeking harmony and peace, the love and compassion, and understanding that we are all sovereign beings?

What If...We Are Not All HERE,

What If...More people were happy with their thoughts, words, deeds, and actions, instead of being negative, grumpy, angry, spiteful, jealous, argumentative, judgmental, guilt tripping, or disrespectful of themselves and others - where would this world be???

Would we be more accepting, caring, and compassionate with ourselves and others?

Where does Competition End and Co-Operation Begin?

When and why did Competition take over from Co-Operation?

With all the information platforms that we have today, such as Facebook, Twitter, Tik Tok, etc., does this make people or humanity believe more strongly that we need more competition?

Why is it acceptable that the broadcasting companies are producing and scripting more "Reality" type shows with people who have lots of money, fame, and power?

Is it to keep all who are interested in these types of shows disconnected from one another?

My personal perspective is that these shows are all about the Ego. Insanity really; the name of the game is called separation, deception, cruelty to others, name calling, dis-respect - not to mention all the mental and physical harm that goes around as Competition. Really, why is it that more humans today are mentally ill?

Why don't the Producers of shows actually produce a Reality show that was all about "Real" people like the Dalai Lama, or perhaps people who are having a hard time here or people who channel; or how about people who can achieve what others call "Miracles?"

What about people who are investigating the truth of what is really going on with this planet and Universe, with having their perspectives and understandings open for all who are intrigued with what

'Cause We Are Not All THERE.

they have discovered? The one channel that I know that does have this information is called GAIA TV. I really love this channel.

I found this channel when I was looking for more shows done by Dr. Steven Greer, and I am so grateful for Gaia TV. This is an avenue of greater understandings, instead of watching the negative programming around the news channels, or reality shows, etc...

What If...Love was the only constant in this world instead of Change?

Change happens in every moment of our lives. Think about this for a moment. What you were thinking about 1 or 2 seconds or minutes ago has changed to something else. Some things change so that we can learn from the experience to become more whole as a human being. Some things come from our sub-consciousness so that we have the opportunity to use our senses and our perspectives to see the truth, or perhaps have a greater understanding of any given situation or circumstance.

When Love is added to the cauldron of the Great Spirit within us, there is an energy that is amplified out through our aura (our Energy Body). This energy is felt by everything and everyone we come into contact with during that moment.

Love of Self is where it all begins. Love the Spirit that you are and have always been.

'Cause We Are Not All THERE.

What If...The saying, "When I see it, I will believe it" was changed to "I Believe it, and now I Can See it." Once you believe in something or someone, you will see it, whatever it is.

There is always the common denominator called "The Law of Action" which states:

"This must be applied in order for us to manifest things on Earth.

Therefore, we must engage in actions that support our

thoughts, deeds, dreams, emotions, and words."

This also applies to "The Law of Cause and Effect" which states that,

"Nothing happens by chance or outside the Universal Laws.

Every action has a reaction or consequence"

and "We Reap what we have sown."

In other words, if you are doing your very best to be compassionate, have mindful conversations in a loving manner, for the highest and purest good, you will then be provided the opportunity to believe that there are millions of possibilities and probabilities that will occur, according to your mindset. Then you will SEE things unfold right before your eyes.

What If...We Are Not All HERE,

What If...This lifetime, or for that matter, all lifetimes, (being as they all exist and correspond together) are all puzzle pieces?

With all our experiences, understandings, perspectives and learning lessons that we create in all our moments, are we here to figure out how each puzzle piece fits into another?

Do we miss or ignore some of the pieces that would place us even higher on our evolutionary platform?

Do we dismiss our real truths from our hearts and follow our Ego instead?

Do we really have choices, or do others influence us?

Can we tell the difference?

Are we sometimes blinded by life's situations and not seeing the forest through the trees?

'Cause We Are Not All THERE.

What If...We were never meant to be rushing around like chickens with our heads chopped off?

What ever happened to stopping to smell the flowers?

What happened to taking our time to get to our destinations safely without harm to others?

What is being accomplished with this kind of behaviour?

Does this serve a purpose?

Do you think about your actions and the reactions of others?

Why do we have the mind set of "I have to be first in line?"

Why this madness? Why frustration and anxiety?

Is this about how quickly and easily we judge ourselves and others?

Is this possibly a lesson in Observation in all of our moments?

There have been many instances where I have been driving somewhere at the speed limit or just slightly above the posted sign and other drivers pass me as if I am standing still and there is oncoming traffic. From my perspective, these people are either in so much hurry to get to where they need to be that they don't think about their own lives, or anyone else's.

There have been many people in my life who have said to me "Why would I have chosen this life and my family"! All I can say is that we have ALL chosen to be here, on this planet, in this Universe, at this time. Why not make the very best of it and go within yourself to find out what you are here to understand.

What If...We Are Not All HERE,

What If...Every single human being looked in the mirror and saw all the beauty and light of their soul within themselves?

Do you think that this would effect your outer world, and if so, how?

When you look at others would you see the "REAL" beauty that lies within every being regardless of their sex?

Would humanity become more compassionate with itself and others?

Would we all become one with the Universal energies and Laws?

'Cause We Are Not All THERE.

W hat If...Beings who have walked upon this planet like Aristotle, Socrates, Plato, Yeshua (Jesus), Enke, Mother Mary, Mary Magdalena, Gandhi, P'taah, Thoth, Horus, Enoch, Isis, Maat, Mother Teresa, Ganesh, Jacob, Confucius, Buddha, the Dalai Lama, Shakti and Shiva, Lakshmi, Mahatmagandi, Martin Luther King Jr., Malcolm X, Rosa Parks, John Lennon, and many, many other human beings throughout history all say the same message, have we really LISTENED to what they were saying?

We need to open our hearts, and our minds to understand the very essence of who we are, where we come from and where we are going. Do we take it for granted that others will always inform us what are lies or truths?

Do you rely on your heart or gut feelings or do you disregard your thoughts and feelings, locking it away because some may think that you belong in a loony bin?

If you don't listen or pay attention to your (Heavenly) body do you become ill or sick in some way or fashion?

Even though we are in the beginning stages of the 21st Century, why are we still very barbaric towards others and ourselves?

Why are we not learning from our past experiences, whatever they may be?

Why doesn't the greater amount of humanity take responsibility for their thoughts, words, deeds, and actions?

Why are some humans so jaded with this life on this planet?

Does this have anything to do with past-life experiences that they choose to avoid?

What If...We Are Not All HERE,

Is it because society has been programming us to believe in good and evil, right and wrong?

Is it because humanity has to put a label on everything?

Is humanity becoming more or less spiritually aware and attuned then other beings on this planet?

Or does it even make a difference?

'Cause We Are Not All THERE.

What If...Some of the words in our English language have been mis-represented as we converse with others or the way we think?

Do we listen to ourselves when we verbalize our sentences?

An acquaintance of mine once said to me:

"Words cast spells.

That is why it is called

SPELLING.

Words are energy.

Use them wisely."

When we break down some words, would we begin to realize the true meaning and understandings of these words?

For instance, if we break down a few words will there be a clearer understanding of what you bring forth into your life?

Disease – You are programmed to be unhealthy on all 4 body levels (emotional, mental, physical, and spiritual), and all 3 levels of your consciousness, sub-consciousness, and super-consciousness.

Dis-Ease – By changing this wording, brings about the meaning that our bodies are not balanced, when we meditate, bring joy and happiness into our lives, we can change the dis-ease to Ease and Grace.

Alone – Many humans feel that they are all alone; they have no one who understands their situation, or their life.

All One – By changing this word and adding one more l, you now will have the understanding that WE ARE ALL ONE.

What If...We Are Not All HERE,

Fear – We have been programmed with Fear, and throughout many lifetimes. We are in Fear of something happening, or we Fear the worst will happen.

Fear – Let's break it down:

F – FALSE

E – EVIDENCE

A – APPEARING

R – REAL

Do you recall the saying that goes: "You have nothing to fear but fear itself?" So, if it's not real, it must be an illusion.

Nothing – We are programmed with this word sometimes as not being able to accomplish things in our lives.

No Thing – Meaning there is absolutely NO THING that can stop us from gaining new perspectives, outlooks, happiness, joy, laughter, and love, all that we really feel is needed for the wonders of this lifetime.

These are just a few examples that I have been working with. I bet that when you put your heart into it, you will come up with more words. Here's a challenge for you - how many words and understandings can you change to help yourself, and others, re-format thoughts, words, deeds, and actions? I would love to hear your results.

'Cause We Are Not All THERE.

W hat If...We were taught to understand from the very beginning of this Earthly experience that each and every human was a Spiritual Being having a Human experience?

What is the definition of the word HUMAN and what does it really mean?

The word Human comes from 13th century French, most likely from the Latin word: Humanus. This word means: Man of the Earth.

We are the Light measurement of vibration or frequency that emits "Hues" and to manifest into a physical form.

With knowing this information now, would we be more respectful of others regardless of their race, color of skin, sexual orientation, language, nationality, or even religious orientation?

What If...We Are Not All HERE,

What If...When you were younger and people would ask what you wanted to do with your life did you have an answer?

Did you know what would fill your heart with joy at your place of work?

I recall many times per week being asked that question, and now that I am many years past my teenage years, I still don't know what I want to do when I grow-up; for that fact, I don't really want to grow-up. I love being me and knowing who I am. Right now I am working on being the kindest, most caring, and compassionate human that I can be, without harming myself or others while keeping myself grounded, self-reliant, and my personal power intact with all the self-esteem that I can carry and hold.

I like to call myself ABI-normal, from the movie Young Frankenstein; I loved the comedic timing of Marty Feldman.

My mantra is:

"Happy people are Healthy people.

Shift happens, so just go with the Flow,

and you will see your new perspective Grow."

There have been many people in my life who helped me grow emotionally, mentally, physically, and spiritually. I am very blessed that when someone needs to get things off their mind and speak to me about their trials and tribulations, I am there for them. I am grateful that these situations allow for my personal growth and advancement while helping others.

'Cause We Are Not All THERE.

What If...Every person who helped you along your way and your day, received a Heart-felt "Thank-you?"

What happens when you open a door for someone?

What kind of response do you get?

There are times when I will open a door for someone, and they will say Thank-you, but most of the time I get either a funny look, or they just walk by me as if I am invisible!

What ever happened to courtesy?

In my opinion, I think this entire world needs more of us to be thankful and grateful towards one another and to stop taking things for granted. It doesn't matter whether it's something big or small.

Do you only help another because you want something in return?

Do you help because you can and it brings you joy or happiness?

Do you expect to be paid back in any way, shape, or form?

Is it a part of who you are that you choose to be kind and helpful to others?

What If...We Are Not All HERE,

What If...We all get what we have asked for at any given moment?

What do you receive?

What do you give back, or do you give back?

Are you very specific with your asking?

For example: I have met many women who are pregnant and I always ask if they know if they are having a boy, or a girl. I would say that about 80% of the time the response has been "I don't care just as long as they are healthy and strong!"

What if that was all that you have asked for, and when the baby is born, yes it is healthy and strong and has Down Syndrome for instance, what happens then?

Does the mother blame herself that it was something she did or didn't do?

Does the father blame himself that it was his sperm?

Is there a genetic malfunction somewhere in their heritage or family lineage that they would be blaming?

Why do we feel the urge to "Blame" something or someone?

Is this fate or karma playing around with us?

Was it because someone made fun of someone else or someone who had Down Syndrome?

Or maybe it happened because you were not being specific with all the details of what you really wanted?

Another possibility is that you have chosen this experience for a clearer understanding, to help others with as well. There is always a

'Cause We Are Not All THERE.

Reason and a Purpose for everything that happens to us and around us.

Are you choosing to be the Cause or the Effect in your moment by moment life?

Another example: A question came to me one day "What do you think you really want or need in the next 5 years?"

As I thought about the question, I said "I really would love to purchase a brand new SUV for myself with air conditioning, automatic windows, and that it must be at least a 5 speed Standard, with cloth seats. I let that thought go out to the Universe and did not think of it again. Within 4 years I was provided the opportunity to purchase my very first SUV.

This only confirmed to me that each and every one of us is more then capable of manifesting what we really want with our hearts. When we come from truth, compassion, honesty, and from our heart and gut, we are capable of manifesting all that is for our purest good. We are the Divine aspect of All That Is, so when we stay as positive as we humanly can, we have the ability to manifest and create the most wonderful aspects of our lives that we came here to experience.

It is only the programming that we have been told to believe and makes us think of what is real, what we can touch, taste, hear, or smell, as well as being brain-washed for many generations. It's time to be the amazing magician and miracle worker that we are meant to be.

What If...We Are Not All HERE,

What If...The saying "Variety is the Spice of Life" was changed to "Love and Laughter are the Spice of Life" - would we all be happier people?

At the same time, I beg to ask, what about those who are grumpy and are carrying around a dark cloud over their heads, will they always be grumpy?

Will they ever find the Love and Light to truly grow within themselves?

Would this world turn out to be a better place to live and grow, or would it stay somewhat the same?

What can we learn from being happy with ourselves?

Do others around you get annoyed when you are living in your joy?

Have you ever been asked "Why are you so happy?"

Have you ever been told by your employer that your happiness and cheery disposition is slowing down the production of your job duties?

Why are some people attracted to drama and controversy instead of what makes their hearts warm and sing?

'Cause We Are Not All THERE.

Whatt If...We all understood that each and every one of us is a Spiritual Being having a human/earthly/physical experience and existence in every moment!

Would we look more within our selves if this was taught by our families and our educational systems?

Do you want to really understand who you are, where you came from originally, and where you are going in this Universe?

There are many questions to always ask, and the answers are always available to us when we listen to our hearts, and our guts.

What If...We Are Not All HERE,

What If...Every human was taught at an early age about the Universal Laws, or as some call it "God's Laws"?

What would this world be like?

Do you know what the Universal Laws are?

Can we all live by them?

Would this world become more harmonious?

What if we all studied the Universal Laws - would we do our very best to live by them? Have greater understanding of our purpose for this life that we have granted ourselves to experience?

By studying and working with the Laws in your day to day, moment by moment experiences, how will they affect your perspective in any given situation that arises throughout your day?

Are you willing and ready to take charge of your life, including taking complete responsibility with joy and peace, to become a positive energy attractor, or would you prefer to be more on the negative hum drum, poor me syndrome that is the programmed being that you may currently be?

When you are ready and willing, you will find that your perspective on events happening around you will change your way of life. It may or may not change another's, but you will understand how powerful you really are.

There are many Hermetic or Universal Laws, so I will give you some of the examples that I work with:

The Law of Divine Oneness:

Helps you to understand that we all live in a world that consists of Energy and Frequencies, and that we are connected to everything.

'Cause We Are Not All THERE.

Everything we say, do, think, and our belief systems affect everything and everyone around us including the Universe.

The Law of Vibration:

Everything in this Universe moves, vibrates, and travels in circular patterns, and it's this principal of vibration that is applied to this physical world with our thoughts, feeling, desires, and our Will in this Etheric world.

The Law of Action:

This is applied when we are manifesting things on this Earth plain. In order to manifest, one must engage in the actions that support our thoughts, dreams, emotions, and words.

The Law of Correspondence:

This is the law of physics and principals that explain our physical world with energy, light, vibration, and motion that correspond with the Etheric and Universe energies. This is where we use that statement "As Above, So Below."

The Law of Cause and Effect:

Nothing happens by chance or outside of the Universal Laws. Every action has a reaction or a consequence; therefore "We Reap What We Have Sown."

The Law of Compensation:

This is where the above mentioned law is applied to our blessings and abundance that are provided for us. These visible effects are provided to our deeds and are given as gifts, money, inheritances, friendships, and blessings.

The Law of Attraction:

This is where we demonstrate how we can create things, events, and people who come into our lives though our thoughts, words, feelings, and actions that produce energies which attract like energies back to us. For example: Negative energy from you attracts negative energy back to you. Positive energy from you attracts positive energy back to you.

In other words, as a **quote from Thoth**:

"Thoughts are the essence of all human creation,

so thoughts are your medium of travel,

Manifesting and healing.

One thought is as POWERFUL as the whole UNIVERSE,

ONE THOUGHT,

ONE MIND,

UNITY CONCIOUSNESS.

One thought can manifest into an illness or disease.

One thought can erase it.

The Power of Your Mind knows NO LIMIT."

'Cause We Are Not All THERE.

The Law of Relativity:

This is where each person will receive a series of problems (or tests if you like) for the purpose of strengthening the LIGHT within your very being. These tests are to challenge us to remain connected to our hearts when working on solving the problem set before us. This also provides us with the opportunity to compare our problems with others to give us another perspective on our situation.

The Law of Gender:

Everything has masculine (yang) and feminine (yin) energies and this is the basis of ALL creation. As Spiritual Beings, it is very important for all to balance the masculine and feminine energies within ourselves so that we can move forward in our evolutionary paths.

What If...We Are Not All HERE,

What If...Every being treated others with the kindness and respect that they themselves are looking for?

No matter what is happening in your personal surroundings or space, does your smile or laughter change the energy around you?

Does this energy uplift you and others?

One of the best things that I witness every day when I am in public is that I enjoy smiling and asking another how their day is going. I would say that at least 95% of the time, I get a smile back and the other's response varies from *it's okay, great, how are you today*?

Would this attitude change your perspectives on your life?

I have also adopted a saying from a former mentor of mine and that is:

"*Every day is a good day;*

some days are just better then others."*

'Cause We Are Not All THERE.

What If...Duality has a significance and purpose in our lives?

Is there really a dark side and a light side of the moon within each and every being on this planet?

Is the dark side a part of our Ego?

Are they the skeletons in our closets we want to ignore?

Does the dark side of us just want to be acknowledged and understood so that we as physical beings may go forward in our healing processes and our spiritual growth?

What are the lessons and understandings that we receive in every moment of our lives whether we are awake or sleeping?

Where does the balance of duality come from?

When we take full and complete responsibility for our own lives, does that bring about the balance that is needed to evolve?

What is really the meaning of all the anxiety, fears, threats, upheavals, lack of self-worth and self-love, injustice, harmony, peace, kindness, compassion, communication and everything else going on with this planet,?

What are our choices?

Do we stay on this planet to find out How Good it can Really Get?

Or do we decide that all we really want is to Get Off this Crazy Ride?

What If...We Are Not All HERE,

What If...The purpose of Marriage was no longer needed and necessary?

Why do some people think: when I have the legal document in my hand, I now own this person's life? They will obey my every command?"

I was married in May of 1988, and my now ex-husband (I left this situation December 1990), before we were married seemed to be a kind person but a little controlling as well. Right after we signed the marriage certificate, I felt like I became a piece of furniture. I was working during the day for a big business in the office, and he was working afternoon shifts. Everyday when I got home from work the telephone would ring (this was a land line phone, before cell phones were created) and if I didn't answer the phone by the 2nd ring, I knew that when he got home he would keep me awake all night.

There were many other things that went on in this relationship. But, I do need to add that he was one of my greatest teachers in this life. He taught me about the kind of relationship that I really wanted. I wanted a loving partnership filled with laughter, communication, and the occasional argument, just to keep the spice of life in the relationship.

I understand that everything happens for a reason, nothing is by chance, but you have to ask yourself, why in the world would I create a relationship like this??? With all the understandings and research that I have acquired throughout this lifetime, at least for now, I have to ask....How Much Better Can It Get!!!

So I must ask: why do we need to be married?

Why can't we just be happy living together, and if one wants to leave the relationship, then one should leave and split all assets instead of one person in the relationship getting everything and the other nothing!

I have witnessed many relationships that have been together for 20+ years, have a wonderful family together. Their children asked the

'Cause We Are Not All THERE.

parents why they were not married, and thought that maybe it's time to get married. For some reason, I think that little piece of paper did something to their minds and hearts, because a few years later, they got divorced!

My point is, if you are in a committed relationship, love and respect one another, why do you think you need to be married?

What If...We Are Not All HERE,

What If...Everyone held the same thoughts and understanding as in my saying, "Your opinion of me is NONE of my business?"

To me, this means: If you like me, great; if you don't like me, well, that's your problem.

Why are some humans desperate to be liked by others?

Is it from self-loathing or self-chastisement, or lack of self-love?

Why is it necessary for some humans to think that everything needs to be done their way only?

Why are the opinions of others so prominent in our lives?

Why are some humans trying very hard to have a fake life?

Why can't we see the beauty in every soul we pass by?

Do you ever take a moment to see the real beauty in another being, let alone yourself?

What do you see, hear, or feel about that other being or yourself?

Do you judge others on their appearance?

Does a person's appearance by the way they dress, or how big or small their physical body structure, offend you?

If so, why are you offended?

Why is it important to you how others make you feel and think?

'Cause We Are Not All THERE.

What If...We connect to Mother Earth with our friends and family members, our guides, our ancestors, our angels, our galactic families, etc. - would we then finally realize that we are ONE?

Nowadays, there are so many avenues or rabbits holes to go through. You can find almost any form of channelers like Lee Harris with the Z's, Darryl Anka with Bashor, Shelia Gillette with the Theo Group; or you can check out Reuben Langdon with his show: Interviews with Extra Dimensionals.

One of my mentors told me years ago to always have a glass of water by my bedside. As soon as I put my feet on the floor, drink the entire glass of water while thinking, *"I ground myself to the Crystal Iron Core Energy of Mother Gaia (Earth). Thank you Crystal-line energy from our water sources that help to heal, and rejuvenate all the energies needed and necessary into my physical body."*

Daily mantra:

"Kind thoughts, kind words, kind deeds, kind actions.

I am Willing to become the very best that I can,

and love all the moments that follow

my footsteps along my path to liberation.

I am a creative, energetic, vibrant, and worthy being,

with all my dreams to become magical,

balanced, harmonious, compassionate, caring,

and healing with myself and others."

THE EGO

'Cause We Are Not All THERE.

W hat If...Our minds were like our vehicles that we drive daily?

Let's say, we have just purchased our very first, brand new vehicle. The first time we sit in the vehicle we notice that new car smell (all those wonderful chemicals), we look at all the buttons, we feel the seat and the comfort of it. With the keys in hand, we start the vehicle to hear the engine roar. We touch all the buttons by turning them on and off to get a sense of how everything works.

Finally, we take our vehicle home, we care for it by giving it regular washes, replace the fluids when they need to be changed, so on and so forth.

Then, many years later, your vehicle has over 300,000 miles/kms on it and the parts are becoming fatigued. Your expenses for repairs are becoming too much to take in. So why is it that the human response is to quickly get rid of our problems instead of working on repairing the issue(s)?

When we pay attention to the clicks and sounds of our vehicle and notice that something is out of balance, we then take it to a mechanic or sell said vehicle.

So, my question is, why has humanity been so quick to rid oneself of issues that the mind has created that requires us to further investigate, understand, or to learn the lessons that have presented themselves to gain more wisdom?

Would this be a part of why we have issues regarding suicides?

Would this be why humanity has become jaded in many aspects that these life experiences have to offer?

We all choose to be birthed into this life for whatever growth our souls have chosen. At the same time, we have also chosen 'Free Will' to experience love, compassion, balance, and harmony. A fine tuning of energies and frequencies one might say.

What If...We Are Not All HERE,

So, why is it that we are being brainwashed to think that if we ignore any kind of disharmony within our bodies, it will eventually go away?

The Buddha taught that the mind is not the brain. The brain is a physical object that we can see, photograph, test, and be operated on with surgery. The mind and the ego can not be seen or photographed. The mind and the brain are different entities. The mind is a formless, non-physical continuum that functions to receive and understand objects. Knowledge comes from the mind, and the mind can go anywhere with just one thought, where the brain does not function this way at all.

With this being said, the mind and the ego are non-physical, formless functions that we have incarnated with as a part of who we are, so this makes me wonder: are these two aspects one in the same, or are they individual expressions from one source eg: good/bad, positive/negative?

'Cause We Are Not All THERE.

What If...All of us were taught at a very early age to check our Ego at the door before we enter?

What would happen if you said to your Ego, "I love you, but I don't have to like you right now, you need to take a back seat on this ride for a little while." Even thinking "I surrender my Ego to the Joy of my Soul." Could these thoughts put a smile on your face?

Is the possibility of the Ego only a 3rd dimensional reality that we have come here to learn and get along with?

Is the Ego here to help us learn our lessons that we came here to achieve, while moving to the next level of our evolution?

Would everyone be able to keep their Egos in check, meaning that you go through your life without your Ego telling you what to do or say about anything or anyone?

Would people become more humbled with their thoughts, words, deeds, and actions if everyone understood the amazing energies and the power of these energies that flow to us when our Ego is being helpful in any given moment?

Would there be more people on this planet willing to help heal our Mother Earth, help heal others emotionally, mentally, physically, and spiritually?

Would they think that they are special allowing their Egos to lead them astray, because all they are looking at is the bottom line, at how much money they will make, despite harming another?

What If...We Are Not All HERE,

What If...Your Ego is the one running your life?

What is the meaning of Ego, from the so-called gods' expectation of humanity?

Did these so-called gods want humans to Eliminate the God/Goddess within ourselves?

Did these gods want humanity to understand that they are more powerful?

Therefore we must worship them or they shall smite us and our families.

How can we change our circumstances?

My personal response to that is that EGO stands for:

Everything Grows Onward

Does our Ego control us with promises of greed, having everything we want because we can, while leaving nothing for anyone else?

Or does our Ego stifle us into thinking that we are not worthy of any kind of abundance, joy, and happiness, to be able to manifest all that our souls desire to create in this incarnation?

'Cause We Are Not All THERE.

What If...Yeshua (or Jesus) was mis-quoted when he said "Step behind me, Devil" - did he mean "Step behind me, Ego?"

I think that we are all run by our Egos to a certain extent and possibly some more than others.

I have learnt that by choosing to come from understanding, integrity, impeccability, love, truth, honesty, and learning that the lessons that I have experienced, my Ego has less control over me.

The more I choose to go within for understanding, the more I am in control of my Ego, by allowing aspects to be acknowledged and released. There have been many times that my Ego still wants to take the helm. Sometimes I need to tell my Ego that it needs to be quiet and when I am ready, I will ask for assistance.

What If...We Are Not All HERE,

What If...We were all taught about the workings of the Negative Ego, how we get immersed into thinking that we are the Superior being over others with the traps we find ourselves in, and what is the best way to become One with our Ego?

It seems like humanity has had a battle going on for hundreds of thousands of year in this Earth cycle. What is an Ego Trap or Trip and how can we become more aware of the pitfalls that lay before us?

If you think it's more "Spiritual" to listen to classical music or soothing nature sounds, and then judge others who choose to listen to mainstream, heavy metal, or pop music, you are in an Ego Trap or Trip.

If you think it's more "Spiritual" to do yoga, become a vegan, buy organic foods, purchase healing crystals, practice any form of healing, meditation, wear hippie/thrift shop clothing, visit Ashrams and read enlightenment/spiritual books, and then start to judge another for not following your lead, you are in an Ego Trap or Trip.

Always be aware of the feeling of being superior to yourself and others. If you are being Self-Righteous, this is your biggest clue that your Ego and Negative thinking or Negative Programming has you trapped.

Your Ego loves nothing more than to be the center of attention and is always at your back door. Your Ego will take any idea and twist it around to serve its own ends by making you feel superior to others. You will start to look down upon those who are not following your Self-Righteous path.

The biggest identifiers are: Superiority, judgement, condemnation, blaming, fighting/war, and all forms of fear, hatred, thinking that the human collective is separate from one another, jealousy, intolerance - the list is long.

How can we become strong, as well as see our Ego as a part of who we are?

'Cause We Are Not All THERE.

Our strong points in this life that have become more balanced in me are: humbleness, integrity, impeccability, vulnerability, keeping our word, having kindness and compassion, believing in our abilities that we create and co-create everything that happens, understanding that we are all brothers and sisters, that we are only different aspects of the Oneness, including our Ego. This list again is long and vast when you take the time to think about what is placed before you.

You can accomplish any task in a loving and nurturing manner and still be strong. It's time to realize how special and unique we all are, that we truly have always been Sovereign Beings.

RELIGION

'Cause We Are Not All THERE.

What If...All the Religions on this planet joined together with their teachings?

Would there ever be a need for any kind of Religious Wars?

Why are there such extreme battles for ownership of the human soul?

There is one major theme with all religions that we can see and hear, and that is they ALL believe in a Supreme Being/Creator of All That Is. So what's the fuss about?

Why is it that all religions believe that God is masculine (man) energy that is vengeful and spiteful if you disobey rules?

With my research, I have found that the Agnostics and the Templers call the Creator the Divine Mother Sophia. Some of the Indigenous cultures call it the Great Spirit. As far as I understand things, this being is the Father, the Mother, and the Child in with what is called the 'Holy Trinity.' This Divine Spirit is within all of humanity as well as within our space brothers and sisters; everything in creation right down to the atom comes from the Divine Spirit.

Has the masculine energy been ruling this planet anywhere from the last 12,000 to 500,000 years, and is it because of this that it's said that God is a man?

Was the feminine energy given any credence or thought of at all when the masculine energy became dominant?

After all, isn't it the feminine energy that gives birth whether they are in animal or human form that creates new life forms?

It's been stated that Mother Mary was a virgin when she became pregnant with Yeshua (or Jesus as it is said in the scriptures). Apparently,

What If…We Are Not All HERE,

Mother Mary was pregnant without the use of a man and his sperm to become pregnant and continued on having 6 or 7 more children with Yehosef (Joseph).

Where did the name Jesus come from if his name was Yeshua?

What if other Religions followed the steps that Paramhansa Yogananda took when he created the Self-Realization Fellowship temple in California in the 19th century?

This temple was created for the purpose of all religions to come together in peace and harmony, to honor another's point of view. At this temple, the daily teachings are not only the Buddhists traditions, but all traditions.

Even the Jewish religion believes that they are the chosen ones. Now, if you look at this from another point of view – aren't we all, regardless of our belief system/structures, faith, or religion, the chosen ones?

Aren't we all spiritual beings having a human/physical experience, in this beautiful school house called Earth?

Aren't we all the Saviours that we have been waiting for?

Why are we taught to believe that there will only be one being that comes to this planet to save humanity?

What if it's every being right here and right now that has the choice to save ourselves?

'Cause We Are Not All THERE.

What If...You believed that we all come from the same Source and we will all return to the same Source?

Do you believe there are some humans who are more spiritually evolved than you are because they are a preacher, minister, pope, priest, guardians of the "Bible" of sorts?

Do you believe that humans who go to church are more superior then the humans who don't believe in going to church?

Do you believe that "Divine Intelligence" is within, instead of outside, your beingness?

Do you believe that you need to go to a special building in order to be accepted, to pray, or to be a God-Fearing person?

Why do we need to fear God in the first place?

It has been stated that "God/Goddess" is kind and loving, father/mother energy, so why on Earth would we need to Fear this being for any reason? We are all created in the likeness and image of God/Goddess, therefore, the God/Goddess energy resides within all of us.

I was watching the news one morning; reporters were talking about a new Pope to be elected. They had a spotlight on the crowd and were interviewing people about how a pope has not been elected yet, and one lady said, with tears running down her face, "If we don't get a new pope soon, this world will go into chaos, and things will never be right again."

My perspective of this is: How easily the human is brain-washed to believe that one person rules this world. We all come from the same energy source and we will all go back to that energy. We are all divine in our own right, and it's time for each and every one of us to proclaim our beingness with love and kindness. There is not one being who should be placed upon a pedestal above and beyond another being. We all deserve to be the unique selves that we were created to be.

What If...We Are Not All HERE,

What If...The story of Adam and Eve originally came from LeMuria?

According to the story, Adam and Eve had 2 sons; there is no mention of any daughters. These 2 sons' were called Cane and Able. Apparently Cane slew Able.

Without Adam and Eve having any daughters, how did the population expand from 3 people?

Did Cain have sex with his mother?

Where they androgynous like the LeMurians?

Where there other sources of beings from other planets that helped to expand human beings on this planet?

Things that make you go....hummmmm.

'Cause We Are Not All THERE.

What If...The forbidden fruit that Adam and Eve ate in the Garden of Eden was not an apple?

The Book of Genesis tells us that Adam and Eve shared a forbidden fruit; this specific fruit was never identified. So where did the apple come from?

There are some Biblical scholars, who believe that the fruit was a fig, and it has been stated that after Adam and Eve ate the fruit, they sewed fig leaves together to cover themselves.

Why did they feel the need to cover themselves when they had the freedom to be as they were, natural in all its beauty?

What brought on this shame of the body, and why are we still like this today?

I can understand that in different parts of the world, where we have colder weather, it is very important to wear warm clothing, but in this so-called Garden of Eden, it has been written that it was beautiful all the time, and there would have been no need for any form of coverings or clothing.

So, is this when our brain-washing, control, and deceit was implanted into our mind-thoughts, or was this story made up for the purpose of control only?

What If...We Are Not All HERE,

What If...Adam and Eve were not just Adam and Eve, as a single couple, but possibly a collective group of beings that inhabited this planet?

What if there was a possibility of Amanda and Eve, or perhaps, Adam and Steve?

What if Eve was not taken from the rib of Adam, but instead, was the other half of Adam, creating the male/female, yin/yang aspect?

How would this change your perspective?

Could it be possible that several groups of beings or entities that started the evolution of humanity or a group of humans were created all at the same time?

What is the real story of life?

How did it all begin?

What if this story in the Bible had a lot of the information taken out from the original scriptures?

What if some of the stories in the Bible have been misinterpreted?

Would the real truth be the ending of any religious control over the populous?

'Cause We Are Not All THERE.

What If...The word "Worship" meant something different than what any one of us has been told?

Does the word "Worship" mean to take your power away?

Has this word been mis-interpreted, and if so, who benefits?

In this timeline for humanity, I would say that it's time now to take back the Oath that was projected upon humanity. As I was working on this book, there was a Divine inspiration that came out through my fingers that stated:

"There is no need to "Worship" any other being any longer.

I understand that when I "Worship" another entity,

I am giving them my power and energy out

of fear, loss, and unworthiness.

I am very Grateful to be blessed with all the

Abundance in all its forms that I create and

co-create with the Divine Intelligence of All That Is.

I am a vibrant being of Love and Light.

I have the Power to Change my perceptions of this life.

I am a Divine Spiritual being having a human experience.

I have all the energy to manifest all that is for my

Highest and Purest Good and for the

Highest and Purest Good for the Universe.

I am connected with the higher aspects of my beingness.

I am worthy of loving myself and others.

What If...We Are Not All HERE,

What If...All the temples, churches, mosques, cathedrals, etc., never needed to be built?

Were they all designed to hold on to the aspect of fear, domination, and confusion amongst the population?

Is it possible that buildings were created on ley lines to enhance ones spiritual awareness?

What if your physical body was the only temple you needed to go to in order to pay homage?

What would occur if every being understood that the temple of the soul and spirit are within your beingness?

All you need is to still the mind and body in meditation to utilize your Divine Intelligence and your heart!

Would this change your perception of Hell or the Devil?

Around 300 A.D., Constantine got some of the religious (Catholic) leaders together with whatever scriptures they had and decided to write the "Bible."

There was a great amount of information that was left out like scriptures from Mother Mary and Mary Magdalena and the reason is that with ancient scriptures being found around the known world some scriptures had not been interpreted at that time, or they only found half of the information. This was a time where the feminine was not allowed a voice at all, and the majority of humanity was illiterate. Accordingly, the Bible was to be placed under lock and key.

They needed to have control and fear tactics so that the populous would follow them. At this time in our history, and for at least the past 12,000 years or more, the masculine energy was running the planet.

'Cause We Are Not All THERE.

This masculine energy came around to extinguish the innate power that the feminine had, because apparently, the feminine energies take away from the masculine energies. Therefore, all females must be controlled by the man of the house. This would also explain why Mother Mary and Mary Magdalena's scriptures are very short stories within the Bible.

Constantine saw that these two women were very powerful in their own divine right. Mother Mary was an Essene, which is another sect of the Jewish religion.

Mary Magdalena came from the territory of Magdalum and was proved financially with her mother's dowry. She was not a prostitute as the Bible says she was. She was the one who financed Yeshua's (or Jesus') travels across the continent. At the time of Mary and Yeshua, the masculine energy dominated the world as we know it; therefore, without Yeshua, Mary Magdalena could not have a voice. Another fact of this story is that they were married and had a family before he went on the cross. I am sure that there is or will be more research done regarding facts and falsities.

As the story goes, Constantine and his mother (Helena) were very close. She was a strong woman mentally, and spiritually, so I think that Constantine admired his mother and at the same time was scared of her, as she was a single parent and somewhat a pillar of strength for him.

Now is the time for all citizens, human beings, life forms, whatever you choose to call yourselves to open up and understand that we are all here for a purpose. I believe that our purpose is to embrace our sovereignty, our soul, our spirit, and to know beyond any shadow of a doubt that we are all created and co-created in the likeness and image of the Divine aspect of All-That-Is.

According to "Yeshua" or "Jesus," he was here at that time to demonstrate to all of humanity that we all have the same capabilities, and power as he had, and that we too can accomplish everything that he has done, or even more. There have been many others throughout the history

What If...We Are Not All HERE,

of the World who have come to this planet to demonstrate our talents and abilities if we choose to accept them and take responsibility for our thoughts, words, deeds, and actions.

So now, will this provide you with all the potential our human existence has to offer with all our possibilities and probabilities and how we are truly endless Divine, Sovereign beings?

'Cause We Are Not All THERE.

What If...We all understood that "DEATH" is only a new beginning, a new birth into another life?

If this is the case, and I strongly believe that it is, why would anyone be afraid or scared of the physical death of the body?

Why do we mourn the way we do?

There are some cultures around this planet where the women wear black for the rest of their time here as a measure of mourning. Why?

I understand that we all mourn the crossing over or death of our loved ones and I have experienced friends and family members setting out to a new life when they are finished with this one regardless of their age. This makes me wonder...why some might spend more years grieving over their loved one's passage of time, than others.

Now, I am not being disrespectful, that is not my intention, but I do wonder why there are some that take death harder then others, and why some people seem to get back to their lives quicker then others. Does it have anything to do with our understanding of life and death (or life and re-birth as I like to say)?

Is it because most religions tell their congregations that death is all about what you do here on this planet?

An acquaintance of mine once stated: "the Bible says that we only live one lifetime on this planet, and to think that we keep coming back is blasphemous, and doing any work such as past-life regression is the devil's work and you will surely go to Hell for that!"

My understanding of past-life work is that we have all lived at least 200 – 250 past lives, possibly more, considering how long this planet, and solar system has been here.

What If...We Are Not All HERE,

According to Hindu and Buddhist tradition, we keep coming back into physical form until we are forever freed from all material longings. From the book: Autobiography of a Yogi, by Paramhansa Yogananda,

"The undeveloped man must undergo countless earthly, astral, and causal incarnations in order to emerge from his/her three bodies."

The scriptures state: (God encased the human soul successively in three bodies – the idea, or causal body: the subtle astral body, seat of man's mental and emotional natures; and the gross physical body). A master who achieves this final freedom may elect to return to earth as a prophet to bring other human beings back to God/Goddess, or like Sri Yukteswar, may choose to reside in the astral cosmos.

Why are we told to be a "God fearing" person?

Why do the clergy promise us, we will go to Heaven if we place our fear in God and repent our sins, but if we are "bad" in their eyes we will go to Hell?

Is there really a Heaven or Hell out there somewhere or is this all a part of the programming and the fear tactics used upon society to control and manipulate?

I wonder, do we create our own Heaven on Earth or our own Hell on Earth and do we really have a choice?

We always have a choice regarding everything that you believe, or don't believe. Every moment is a choice, and even if you choose not to make a choice, you have still made a choice.

There are also many books, movies and documentaries available on Near-Death Experiences. People have been clinically dead, and have come back to life - some have had this experience more than once and have documented those experiences. Dr. Raymond Moody has written many books regarding his studies of Near-Death Experiences. If you

'Cause We Are Not All THERE.

haven't read any of his material yet, you should check it out.

Dannion Brinkley wrote the book "At Peace in the Light." Dannion came back to life after being electrocuted by lightening, a very interesting story. There is also a plethora of information from Edgar Cayce, the Sleeping Prophet.

GOVERNMENTS and POLITICS

'Cause We Are Not All THERE.

W hat If...All the politicians on this planet were run by their Egos? Or are they being controlled as to what they can say and do?

Politicians in this 20th Century are taxing the general working population at every turn. They are coming up with new ways, with, as they say, "Solutions to the Global Problems" to tax us more and more. Will it ever stop?

As it is, the general blue collar worker just makes enough money (per 2 weeks) to get by, meaning they barely have enough money to either pay their mortgage, phone bill, TV or internet bill, water and sewage bills, garbage pick-up, and more. Not to mention any after school activities that their children want to attend.

I would like to know what blue collar worker gets a retirement package of $250,000.00 per year after let's say 5 – 10 years of service, other than the politicians.

Most of the elderly that I know of are barely scraping by with very little education; pension cheques that are barely above poverty; yet they all were very hard workers. I know of many people who had to work 2 or 3 jobs while raising their families, and worked until they were 65 years old. Now the governments want people to work until they are at least 70 years old. What is it going to be like for our children's children?

What kind of legacy are we leaving for them?

If you started working at age 16 while you were in school and worked until you became 65 years young, you will be working for 49 years of your life to benefit the governments and only receive anywhere from $2,000.00 - $3,000.00 per month until you cross-over (die). At the same time, you have provided the government with millions of dollars throughout your lifespan. What's wrong with this picture?

Why are our governments allowed to spend our money needlessly?

What If...We Are Not All HERE,

Why are they allowed to invest our money without our knowledge, and keep the profits for themselves?

When I was younger, I was always told that our governments work for the people.

Do they really?

I beg to differ. I don't think that that statement is true. Has it ever been a true statement?

Did some government official somewhere at some point say that they work for the people knowing that that information was a lie, and by doing so, filled their pockets?

What are your thoughts about this?

Do you care?

Should you Care?

Where will deception lead us and our children's children down the road?

'Cause We Are Not All THERE.

What If…You knew the absolute truth from our Governments and the World Management Team such as the United Nations, or World Health Organization, or the big Pharma-Care Corporations on their plans for humanity?

What if there were no more secrets from anybody, and everything was out in the open and on the table for all to see?

Would we still need Governments or State Officials to run our world for their benefit?

Would every citizen on this planet become mentally, emotionally, physically, and spiritually stable?

Would we really need any Pharmaceutical companies pumping toxins into our bodies or our food sources?

Are the Governments, Pharmaceutical companies, and the FDA all from one government package with different names to confuse the populous?

What If...We Are Not All HERE,

What If...All the inhabitants on this planet started to live in peace, harmony, and love for themselves and for one another?

Would there be any need for war anywhere?

Would this only be the responsibility of our government officials who say they represent the populous?

Do you think that the government officials are really on the general population's side of life, or are they in the position for fame and glory, power and money, or perhaps World domination?

What would happen if all the corporations around this planet stopped digging, drilling, mining, chopping down healthy trees, sending out chem-trails with all the passenger flights that are taking place nowadays and destroying Mother Earth all for the sake of profit?

Who really benefits from all this destruction?

I know many people who work in the oilfield, mining, and forestry industries. I understand that they have bills and mortgages. They all work very hard and long hours to account for their wages. At the same time, they are following the orders of the Elite that always seem to want more and more. What part of this is giving back to our Mother Earth and helping to make things sustainable?

Are any of our government officials truthfully doing anything about all the tasks that they are claiming to accomplish?

Will any of them ever be held accountable for their actions and deeds?

Will any of them take responsibility for lying or being deceitful to the general population?

Or are they just following orders as well?

'Cause We Are Not All THERE.

What If...The governments slashed their benefits and privileges?

What if they slashed some of their employees' wages and salaries?

Why do we need so many Officials running our Government Agencies, and why does each Senator or Official need to have a large staff?

What are they really doing with all the Tax dollars that they receive everyday from every corner of the World?

Why are Government Officials allowed to spend money on their private vacations with their entire families, expensive hotel suites, and flights that are all out of the populous' pocket?

What if they re-thought how they spend our money?

Why don't our Officials spend their own money on any or all luxury items that they want, instead of using what is really needed for the population?

Should all Governments around this planet be accountable for all the monies that are spent, and where they have allocated the monies, as well as informing the populous of all their decisions regarding their spending habits?

Why is it that many of our past politicians have squandered monies received by the populous, been found guilty of such crimes, and have not done any jail time?

When these situations come up in our daily lives, people have been placed in jail until they get a court hearing on their crimes.

Where is the justice in this and will there ever come a time where all Governments will be held accountable for their actions?

What If...We Are Not All HERE,

We, the populous are always being held accountable for our actions by authorities, why is the shoe not placed on the other foot?

'Cause We Are Not All THERE.

What If...This so called "Game of Life" truly was a game?

Who is in control and why?

Is there a puppet master, and what is their plan for humanity?

Are we really living a Free Choice or Free Will World?

Why are so many Politicians looking at placing their ideals on how they want to control humanity?

Why are they trying to take away our Freedom of Speech, the freedom to protest without going to jail?

Is it because they feel that we are a threat to national security, and are they blocking newspaper/news stations from informing the public of their hidden agendas?

Russell Brand is a British comedian/actor, and Pod caster, he has recorded a segment regarding De-Banking that would shock most people, and at the same time, be not surprising. This is a must watch when you can.

Do we really need to understand anything other than co-operation, kindness, love, generosity, communication, happiness, and joyfulness in our moment by moment lives?

What If...We Are Not All HERE,

What If...There was no need to have power over others?

No need for chemical warfare?

No need for biological warfare?

No need for religious warfare?

No need for any kind of warfare on this planet or in this Universe anymore?

Is this how it is in other planetary systems that are in our Universe and Galaxy?

What if by having this mind set and raising our consciousness and awareness with the Collective Mind, we become more co-operative with one another instead of being competitive?

'Cause We Are Not All THERE.

W hat If...Martial Law was abolished and was no longer allowed by any Government Agencies?

Would our lives be better because we have grown and learnt to be at peace with everything around us; would we then need any form of governing agency or bureaucratic policies placed upon society?

Why is it that we as the societies (populous) of this planet are being withheld information?

Our governments seem to think that the population on this planet is stupid and beneath their superiority; therefore, that gives them dominion over everyone, to lie and betray each and every one of us. (So they think).

How and why is that morally justified?

Whatever happened to being ethical?

When will they be speaking the truth?

Or do they even understand what Truth means?

Why does there seem to be big money for the corporations that are involved to destroy our Mother Gaia's (Earth) of valuable resources that are in place for humanity to utilize?

Who really benefits from all the profits that accumulate on a daily basis?

What If...We Are Not All HERE,

What If..."Global Warming" is just Propaganda, and Fear?

There have been many stories throughout the ages regarding the changing weather patterns and how this is the natural cycle of our Mother Earth. Nostradamus quoted in his quatrains that:

> *"Where it was once warm will become cold, and where it was once cold will become warm."*

All these massive events that Mother Gaia (Earth) is creating, is for a reason, for a purpose. This is not the first time that our Earth planet has evolved, nor will it be the last. Mother Gaia goes through transformations, just like any other being. She feels all the emotional upheaval that is created through us; this is partially why natural disasters are occurring all over this planet.

This is a part of our heritage, and lineage. She is going to the 4th and 5th dimensions or densities, whichever you choose to call it, and we are all here in these moments (and YES, we have chosen to be here for this) to understand, and learn. As we raise our consciousness, our vibrations/frequencies, we become more aligned with our Mother Gaia. As our energies rise, we begin to open our hearts, with loving and compassionate energies for her, all her inhabitants, ourselves, and all our brothers and sisters.

For some reason, some of the elite seem to think of themselves and their immediate family members, and that they must rise above all in order to have control.

But, what if this planet only had the elite that are in a life form?

Where would they be?

Would they be the ones that toil the ground for raising crops and animals?

'Cause We Are Not All THERE.

Would they be the ones that have sweat on their brows?

Probably NOT; they would just create robots and computer systems to do all the work for them.

Each and every one of us needs to open our eyes, hear and speak the truth, understand that we are all brothers and sisters. Our Souls and Spirits have the same goal, whether you are financially wealthy or poor. We all need to come together in love and joy, bringing with us the light that we all hold. Together we stand strong, together we have the power. Together we can become one with All That Is, the Divine Intelligence, the Universe, the Multi-Verses, to be the Creators and Co-Creators that we truly are.

Let's look at this from another point of view. Many humans on this planet don't think of Mother Earth as a living, breathing, vibrant being. But guess what, she is.

Humans have been raping and pillaging Mother Earth for hundreds of thousands of years. There has been so much human blood splashed upon her from battles and wars.

Do you think the Earth changes that are happening right now in this 20th century are because Mother Earth needs to cleanse herself, just like we do when we need a shower or a bath?

Why are our governments making so much money off Mother Earth and her natural course of evolution and doing nothing to help her?

Is it because they think they are superior to Mother Earth and that they can tame her just like one would tame a wild animal?

Or is it that some of them think they know what's best for Mother Earth and everyone else?

Now, I understand that there has been some human error with what's happening right now, the ice caps have melted many times before, the land masses at one point I strongly believe was all one land mass.

What If...We Are Not All HERE,

The oceans have their ebb and flow, they rise, and they sink. Tectonic plates move. Winter storms are leaving snow in places that have not seen snow since the last ice age. More hurricanes and tornadoes are going through countries that have never experienced those kinds of winds. Rain forests are being depleted for the human race. Cities are getting bigger with skyscrapers. Small towns are starting to be over run by city folk on the weekends and summer holidays. Cruise ships are getting so big that they can be looked at like a city somewhere, minus motor vehicles.

Another fact about Global Warming is from Billy Carson, I will make this brief so you will need to check out his website called 4BiddenKnowledge.com.

Billy has stated that he was studying Astronomy; he purchased a telescope and was looking out at the night sky when he noticed an anomaly. When he took a clear look into the night sky he discovered that there was another Sun with a brown planet orbiting the Sun. Many years after Billy's discovery, NASA finally confirmed that Billy was right.

The perspective that Billy Carson has was that there is an ebb and flow with this Brown planet and its Sun, and this is creating Global Warming, not just on our planet Earth, but with all the planets in this solar system. For more information on this subject you can access the Awakening Conference 2020 UK, on Gaia TV.

'Cause We Are Not All THERE.

What If...Humanity didn't need any kind of Military operations?

Do we really need to be violent against any being, whether they are born on this planet or not?

Why have our governments, politicians, large organizations and corporations, and the like, been able to make profits from war, while the rest of the planet's inhabitants have to struggle and try to get by on a pittance?

Why would the elite think that war/fighting is needed or necessary?

I have heard the saying "War makes money." For whom does it make money?

Why would our Government Officials and the Heads of the Militaries think that this is all just?

I for one would really like to understand the truth of it all.

What If...We Are Not All HERE,

What If...The majority of humanity understood what the Pandemic (COVID-19) was really about in 2019?

There are many people that I have spoken to that like to call it "The PLAN-demic."

Was this all about how fear tactics can be utilized on humanity?

Was this a world-wide plan by some bio-engineering technicians working on chemical warfare to deplete the population on this planet?

How much money did the Governments and Pharmaceutical companies really pocket from this plan?

Was this an experiment to find out how many people would listen to these so-called medical experts that were paid very handsomely for their efforts by our Governments?

What was really in those vaccinations, and will we ever be told the truth?

Why is it now, 3 - 4 years after this world-wide vaccination program began, there are many more people unexpectedly leaving this planet from severe heart conditions, low and auto-immunity deficiencies, and various other conditions?

Was this really the plan?

This has got to make you ask for some answers?

Why was it ever allowed that pregnant women and new born babies needed this vaccination?

Why were Governments offering tickets to sporting events and the like for the entire population to get this vaccination?

'Cause We Are Not All THERE.

Why were the Governments trying to make this vaccination program a law, and why were they strongly suggesting that those who did get the vaccine would be better off then those that didn't get vaccinated, pitting one against the other?

Did they really think that this kind of bullying would work?

There are many people on this planet that did not fall for this kind of out-worldly behaviour; at the same time, there are still many people still getting up-to-date vaccinations.

What If...We Are Not All HERE,

What If...The Freedom Convoy was successful with what the organizers wanted to accomplish for humanity with the Governments?

In Canada, we had what was called "The Freedom Convoy," the intent of which was, as I understand it, to talk openly and peacefully regarding the Human Rights of the populous and the ability to choose whether or not to be vaccinated instead of being forced (in order to keep your job).

For some reason, the Canadian Officials felt threatened by the common-folk that wanted to make a difference for humanity by standing up to the Government, and of course this was broadcasted around the world.

A while ago I heard that in Ontario, Canada, the Government Officials stated that they were going to start fining protestors with possible jail time. Is all this because of the Freedom Convoy in 2020 that helped to open peoples' eyes around the world?

Why did our Prime Minister, Justin Trudeau go into hiding stating that he had COVID and would not talk to the protestors?

Why did our Prime Minister put these people in jail for supposedly the obstruction of justice and/or being a National Security risk?

Why did our Prime Minister and Christa Freeland have all the banking institutions lock-up bank accounts that had supported this convoy and had a gag order put into place?

What are they afraid of?

At the time of completing this book, there are still a lot of people who have not been allowed any access to their monies (this is Millions of dollars that the Banking institutions and the Governments are withholding) for what?

'Cause We Are Not All THERE.

Is it for the benefit of keeping control over everyone?

What makes us think that our Governments are always providing what is best for the population?

What If...We Are Not All HERE,

What If...Everyone on this beautiful planet, especially our government officials, town and/or city counselors, and the elite property owners, realized that NOBODY owns land on this planet, we are merely caretakers on this land for Mother Earth.

Why are humans being disrespectful instead of appreciating this land?

Why do we need plastics or other garbage thrown around as we drive down our highways?

Why are we all paying astronomical taxes?

Why are hobby farms not allowed to have write-offs like commercial livestock farmers?

I understand that there is a difference between a large farm and a hobby farm, but, and I mean a big BUT, we all have to tend to the animals with grooming, feeding, vet appointments when needed, and nurturing all the animals that are around us.

Why do we need to have town or city approval on a farm to put up structures that are required for proper care for the animals, and everytime you let them know about improvements to your land, they want to see what you are doing and charge you more taxes?

When will this stop?

Is society getting out of control with taxes and who is lining their pockets?

Why do we need so many politicians for each province, territory, state, or area where we are residing?

Why don't they open their ears and listen to what the populous has to say? If we are all to live in a Free Will society, why doesn't our opinion matter to most of the politicians running our countries?

'Cause We Are Not All THERE.

As far as taxes are concerned, why are any and all Government Officials allowed to take extravagant vacations with their entire families somewhere exotic, and have the tax payers pay for their $5,000.00 per night suites?

Why are they allowed these kinds of luxuries when we have our brothers and sisters who have gone into needless battles for their countries, for the freedoms that we should all be grateful for, who are now suffering emotionally, mentally and physically and getting so little in return?

If the common-folk per se, were to follow in their footsteps, I think we would all be in jail for tax evasion or something to that effect.

What are these Governments really doing?

Who are they paying attention to?

What If...We Are Not All HERE,

What If...There really was no difference between Russia and China compared to any other country that runs under a Communist Government?

Why do we need Communism?

The only difference that I can see between any Communist country and ones that say we are Free, is that the Communists are very proud to voice that they are Communist, while the other countries are in denial of being Communist.

Is this all about them being afraid that the general populous will rise up, take a stand together arm in arm against their barbaric ways?

Are they in fear that the general populous will take everything away from them especially their power, and money?

Is the World Management Team in fear of losing control when the majority of the population on this planet finally come together as one voice, one heart, and one consciousness?

I can hardly wait to see what the changes will be. I am completely looking forward to the day and moment when we all have World PEACE, and great respect for everything that this life has to offer.

Right now, in order to achieve World Peace, we must first achieve Inner Peace, harmony, balance, joy, and love.

Either way, this is your life to live, so why not live it to its fullest and happiest! It's time for all of us to be the Divine, Sovereign spark of love and light that we all came here to achieve.

This is NOW the moment we have all been waiting for. Where oneness can reign, where truth, unity, compassion, and love is allowed to flow and grow, ever expanding by opening our hearts and minds to our spirit and our soul's destiny by raising our vibrations and frequencies together as one.

'Cause We Are Not All THERE.

It has been said

"We are the ONE that we have been waiting for."

The choice is yours, what do you choose to do with your life?

What If...We Are Not All HERE,

In Conclusion:

With Love and great Gratitude, we thank you for reading our book; we value your thoughts and perspectives.

If you choose to correspond we can be reached at JoyChild369@gmail.com

Please feel free to send us your comments.

Universal Cosmic Consciousness
(Picture)

'Cause We Are Not All THERE.

ABOUT THE AUTHOR

Many years ago during a reading, I was informed that my Spiritual name is ***Joy Child of the Universe*** that will be used when directed.

In this lifetime, I have been a Metaphysical seeker, teacher, and researcher, always seeking wisdom and understanding from wherever I could find it.

Ever since I was a child, I knew what I was born to do….help others.

With such an early understanding of what was needed to be accomplished through meditation, yoga, visualization, and practice, to master techniques using natural and spiritual ways to help others balance their lives, heal themselves, help to open people's minds and hearts, and now an Author.

What If...We Are Not All HERE,

'Cause We Are Not All THERE.

Manufactured by Amazon.ca
Bolton, ON

43316228R00083